D1324556

GOLD COAST TO GHANA

Colin Russell

Ex Libris

Judy Norall -
given me by Rusty
(Colin Russell's
daughter)

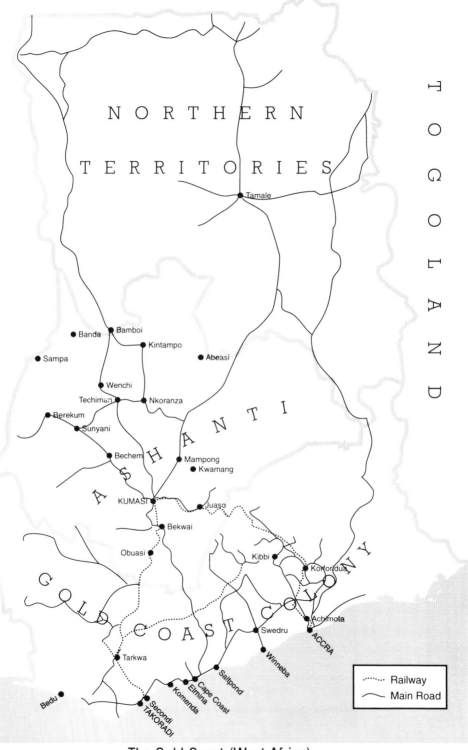

The Gold Coast (West Africa)

Gold Coast to Ghana

A Happy Life in West Africa

ARTHUR COLIN RUSSELL

The Pentland Press
Edinburgh – Cambridge – Durham – USA

© A. C. Russell, 1996

First published in 1996 by
The Pentland Press Ltd
1 Hutton Close,
South Church
Bishop Auckland
Durham

All rights reserved
Unauthorised duplication
contravenes existing laws

ISBN 1–85821-405-X

Typeset by Carnegie Publishing, 18 Maynard St, Preston
Printed and bound by Antony Rowe Ltd, Chippenham

To the memory
of my dear wife, Elma,
and to my three daughters who, since her death
in 1967, have been a continual joy, comfort, and support

Contents

	Illustrations	ix
	Foreword	xi
1	Preamble: Preparing for Service in The Gold Coast	1
2	First Tour: July 1929 – October 1930	8
3	Second Tour: February 1931 – December 1932	18
4	Third Tour: June 1933 – December 1934	27
5	Fourth Tour: May 1935 – January 1937	35
6	Fifth Tour: June 1937 – October 1938	38
7	Sixth Tour: March 1939 – November 1940	45
8	Seventh Tour: September 1941 – July 1943	56
9	Eighth Tour: February 1944 – May 1945	64
10	Ninth Tour: December 1945 – June 1947	71
11	Tenth Tour: January 1948 – April 1949	81
12	Eleventh Tour: October 1949 – February 1951	87
13	Twelfth Tour: July 1951 – October 1952	89
14	Thirteenth Tour: January 1953 – May 1954	96
15	Fourteenth Tour: October 1954 – July 1955	101
16	Fifteenth Tour: October 1955 – July 1956	104
17	Sixteenth and Last Tour: October 1956 – May 1957	115
	Appendices	137

Illustrations

Map of the Gold Coast	Frontispiece
Christiansborg Castle	21
Christiansborg Castle – Dining Room and Punkah	23
Cape Coast Castle	28
Elmina Castle	29
Kumasi, the daily market	40
Kumasi Durbar, the Silver Drums	41
Wenchi, D.C.'s bungalow	45
Bamboi Ferry	47
Kofi Genfi's family	52
Kumasi Durbar, 1946	74
Kumasi Durbar, 1946. Asantehene and the Golden Stool	75
South Togoland Council (with Mrs. Russell and self)	92
Government Lodge, Cape Coast, with Mrs. Russell	93
The Residency, Kumasi	104
Kumasi, C.A.A.'s Office, Self, 1956	106
Seating plan for a dinner party given for M.P.'s prior to Independence	111
Kumasi, visit of Secretary of State	117
Kumasi, the crowds at the Secretary of State's visit	118
Kumasi, the Fort	121

Order of Parade, the Queen's Birthday Parade, 20th April,
    1957   125

Kumasi, the Race Course. Asantehene with Mrs. Russell
    and self   127

Letter from the Prime Minister, Kwame Nkrumah   130

At the Railway Station   132

On the train. Bridget with Mrs. Russell and self   133

Foreword

THE BASIS FOR THIS MEMOIR is a fairly complete set of daily diaries. Their main fault is that they record chiefly social and recreational matters, and only occasionally any official activities. This bias has been corrected by recourse to a vast number of copies of official papers in my personal collection. I brought these home with me in 1957 and, having made use of them, intend to deposit them with the University of Science and Technology in Kumasi, Ashanti.

The following pages were written primarily for my daughters. Over the years, however, I have often recounted what I thought were amusing stories of my life in the Gold Coast, now Ghana, and rightly or wrongly, many people have asked me to commit these to writing. What follows is the result.

I hope, first and foremost, that these pages will be of interest to my family and, perhaps to a number of my friends. I would like to hope, secondly, that it may be of interest to those whom I do not even know, who wish to learn more about the colonial Gold Coast and its transition to independent Ghana.

And finally, in preparing these memoirs, I have been greatly helped by Professor Wilks and his wife, Dr. Nancy Lawler, who not only travelled twice from Wales to Angus to see me, but also typed my scarcely legible scrawl. They later included numerous additions and amendments which I sent them. Professor Wilks is sometimes called the modern "R.S. Rattray" and undoubtedly writes with knowledge and authority on Ashanti, both its history and its culture, so it is clear what a debt I owe to him and his wife.

A. C. Russell
Balgavies Lodge
Forfar, Angus
1996

CHAPTER I

Preamble: Preparing for Service in The Gold Coast

W hy do I call it a "Happy Life in West Africa"? I spent 28 years in the Gold Coast, renamed Ghana after it became independent in 1957. The following pages tell of those years, spent mainly amongst the once dreaded warrior "Ashantees", though in my time they were reconciled to accepting the benefits of western civilisation – communications, education, hospitals, etc. – which the United Kingdom was constantly trying to improve, perhaps slowly, but at least steadily. Tribal wars had ceased, there was ample food, and the happiness of the people of Ghana was what made my life there a happy one.

It all began when I was at Oxford, contentedly reading law at the Honours School of Jurisprudence, as it was called, with every likelihood of becoming a solicitor and entering my father's legal firm in Edinburgh. Then, during my second or third year, in or about 1927, many undergraduates became excited by Colonial Office advertisements asking for youngsters to join the Colonial Service. In recent years the great majority of people going abroad seem to do so principally to 'give service,' and secondly, to have an interesting time. In my day, however, it was the other way round. Naturally, the bulk of those chosen had learnt at school that those who have should give to those who have not, but undoubtedly it was the thought of Africa's "wide open spaces" that appealed to me. Like many others, I put down Kenya as my first choice and Northern Nigeria as second.

I do not actually remember applying or being interviewed – for most of us our School and College records would be sufficient. In due course I received an offer from the Secretary of State – it was to serve in the Gold Coast. I still remember my Mother's instant reaction: "You will, of course, refuse." To her West Africa was 'The White Man's Grave,' where missionaries went and died in large numbers, and where merchants went to make money but also to die in large numbers. And indeed, in 1929, though no longer the White Man's Grave, the Gold Coast was still a place of ill-health. Of the six of us who were on the course at Oxford and went to the Gold Coast, two died on service, two were invalided out of service, and only two of us stayed the course. In 1929, tours in West Africa were planned for eighteen months, with a week's leave for every month served – and the sea voyage in each direction counted neither as service nor as leave. In East Africa, where the climate was generally so much better, tours were longer and leave was only five days per month served. Furthermore, our salary began at £450 per annum as against £400 in East Africa. So West Africa had many advantages. In addition, £450 was very reasonable pay. I tried to save £100 annually and usually succeeded. Briefly, I never regretted accepting, and I had, as I have said, a long and very happy 28 years in the Gold Coast.

All those appointed in 1928 were called 'cadets.' We were sent to Oxford or Cambridge to do nine months' Tropical Training – some 30 to 40 of us at each University – to prepare us for our future responsibilities. Naturally we took our classes seriously, yet often frivolously. For example, we took Surveying and if the Instructor was away, he might return to find us using the marker posts as javelins. As my hobby was hill-walking and climbing, I was well conversant with the use of map and compass. Indeed, many years later, I did make use of what I had learned and, helped by my wife, surveyed a nine-mile road to a village, laying out a new line that cut the distance to six miles.

Another series of lectures was Tropical Health – which, alas, we again took rather frivolously. When our lecturer told us of 'bubonic' plague from which few survived, we smiled, but when he told us of 'pneumonic' plague from which no one recovered, we burst into laughter. (If I have these two the wrong way round, I apologise – but they are Asiatic illnesses, and as we were all going to Africa, we did not feel involved). Another course of study was Native Languages. For those going to Kenya who took Swahili or for those going to Northern Nigeria who took Hausa, the course was commendable, but for those of us going to the Gold Coast there were three main languages in the South and at least three in the North, and as we had no idea where we would be stationed, we did not enthuse. The Legal Lectures were good, for we would all be expected from time to time to sit on the bench as magistrates. I already had a legal degree, and my father (a very wise man – not only did he start the National Trust for

Scotland but also bought those invaluable irredeemable debentures allowing one to have the privilege for all time to buy tickets for the International Rugger matches at Murrayfield), my father in his wisdom thought it would be a help if I studied for the English Bar.

I might here mention that to be called to the English Bar, at least in those days in the twenties and thirties, one kept 'term' by 'eating dinners' – and one of my Oxford friends and I used to try and sit with two Indians, as the custom in my Temple was for each table of four to have a bottle of claret in addition to as much beer as one might wish. As the Indians were always teetotal, my friend and I enjoyed their quota of wine. Bar examinations are usually spread over three or four years, but as I only began the course shortly before going abroad, I used to take an examination each time I came home on leave – so it took me ten years to pass all of them. Truly, it was not just incompetence! In 1939 I found myself the Senior Student and, after being addressed by the Bencher, 1939, Sir John Simon, I would have to reply. It was a daunting task! However, I managed, and indeed was greatly thanked, not for the quality of my words but for their brevity. In the previous term thanks had been given by an Indian (or West Indian) rather loquaciously and High Table and students all missed the first act of their theatre.

A final note on our Tropical Course: it included excellent lectures on Anthropology and Local History; also much needed advice on the development of Local Government. This last looked at the theory of Indirect Rule rather than Direct Rule, that is, how to try and work through local institutions as far as possible. We were also given some notes on native customs such as: "Do not cross your legs when sitting in public," and "Never use your left hand when passing food or drink."

At long last the Tropical Course ended, and we now had to buy the necessary kit. Quantities of it! Left to myself, my only luggage would have been my school trunk and a small suitcase, but now we were advised to buy, and given a substantial grant to help pay for, tin trunks that were intended to prevent access of insects. One was a long trunk to hold uniform trousers unfolded and a dress sword. Two were to hold the rest of our clothing. One was a metal box for our helmets. It was a civil offence for Europeans to be in the sun bare-headed between 8 a.m. and 4 p.m., so we would have a large Wolseley helmet for official occasions, a pith helmet for less formal occasions, with room for possibly a third. Then we had to buy a camp bed and mosquito nets, whether for use in camp or in our bungalow, and a folding table and two folding chairs for use when travelling or, as we said, 'on trek', employing the South African word and not 'safari' as in East Africa. We had to have several lamps, hurricane for use in kitchen, bedroom, etc., and a more powerful one, the 'Tilley', necessary for reading; a tin bath (more comfortable than it sounds); a mass of clothes, tidy suits, shorts, white and khaki, etc., etc., and also crockery, cutlery, china, and kitchen equipment. A water filter was also required, for no water was drunk unless boiled first and then filtered – and then, it being tasteless, we usually drank whisky with soda. This necessitated a gas cylinder, not the tidy one we use today with a sodastream, but what roadmen used – four feet high, weighing 'a ton' but providing enough soda water for a tour of 18 months. Then there were golf clubs, tennis rackets, books to read, and quite a quantity of food such as tinned salmon. The two outfitters recommended to us, one in London, the other in Liverpool, were most helpful, and I do not recollect buying anything not needed.

So to actual departure. I and my Oxford friends were due to sail on 10th July 1929, and this was always a slightly sore point as the Cambridge cadets had sailed a week earlier and so were always a week senior to us. My route was by the comfortable Caledonian Railway, from the Caledonian Station, Edinburgh West End (now a hotel, car park, etc.), to Carstairs. Here we were hitched on to the Glasgow train and, leaving at 10 p.m., would reach Liverpool early next morning. This left time to taxi to the Adelphi Hotel for breakfast and then to wander down to Princes Dock, where Elder Dempster's boat would be waiting, ready to sail at 3 p.m.

We always sailed by Elder Dempster's Line. They had three services a month, leaving Liverpool on Wednesdays. My father very kindly had the *Times* posted to me in weekly bundles – one of them would have twelve editions – and my boy Kwasi placed a copy on my breakfast table daily, a Monday's paper on a Monday, but always five weeks old. This method had the advantage that one did not have to read, "Who will win?", but only "Who did win?" I little dreamt then that 25 years later, in 1954 when in Accra, I would be able to drive to the Airport and actually collect a copy of that day's *Times*. My first trip in 1929 was on the *Appam*. It was a ship of some 7,000 tons and I thought this big, but to those who worked in India or South Africa it was a tiny one. I found it most comfortable; the cabins were good, and we were accommodated two or three of us to a cabin. There were no fans in those days, so after passing the Gambia it became hot at night, and we soon learnt the meaning of "POSH" – port outward, starboard home – to get the best of the offshore wind at night.

I thought the food was terrific. I had always fed well but simply at school, university, or at home, but on the *Appam* we had a huge breakfast, a three or four-course lunch, and at night an enormous five-course dinner. Naturally we wore dinner jackets every night until we reached the tropics, and then we wore cummerbunds, gold for the Gold Coast, green for Nigeria, blue for Sierra Leone, red for the Gambia, and short white jackets. My mind boggled at the thought that the chef had to plan his menus for the double voyage, some 30 days, and not only plan but purchase all he needed ere he left Liverpool, as nothing could be bought later on except some small quantities of fruit and vegetables.

We were encouraged to take plenty of exercise – quoits, table tennis or shuttlecocks and, when it became warmer, swimming in the open air pool. After dinner there was always dancing – not my favourite sport. I usually played bridge (auction bridge as 'contract' had not been invented), and playing threepence a hundred, I often made a shilling, which was enough to pay for a glass of whisky and soda. I also enjoyed the 12 days to the Gold Coast playing chess and reading a great deal. I often read Walter Scott, and I might mention that he has had a huge influence on me – especially *Heart of Midlothian*, where Jeannie Deans walked from Edinburgh to London to obtain a pardon from the Queen rather than tell a lie to save her sister's life.

Playing the bagpipes was another hobby of mine. At Oxford I had associated with many fellow Scots, some of whom were able players of the pipes. I took it up, joined the Scottish Pipers' Society, and in 1929 took my pipes abroad with me and practised frequently on board. The back of the ship – the poop – seemed to be an admirable place for practice as the noise bothered no one. Later, I practised continually in many places in the Gold Coast, often in lonely out-stations, and regularly on St Andrew's Night, 30th November, I used to pipe in the Governor or other guests of honour, and later on pipe in the Haggis.

However, back to the *Appam*. In those days we called regularly at Madeira and Las Palmas, mainly, I believe, to oil (to fill the ship's tanks). At Madeira I acquired a taste for their excellent drink and often, feeling rather extravagant, would buy two bottles of Madeira, costing maybe 6*s.* each. We would call at the Gambia, at its capital Bathurst (now Banjul), but lay in midstream and never went ashore. Then came Sierra Leone's capital, Freetown. In the early years, lying in midstream, we amused ourselves by throwing pennies to the truly aquatic natives who dived for them. In the clear water we could often see the pennies sinking deep down, but they were always retrieved. On later trips I regularly went ashore, as my sister, and later she and her husband, were in Sierra Leone for many years. They would always meet the Elder Dempster boat and take me out to Lumley Beach for a swim and a picnic lunch.

Only once did I call in at Monrovia, capital of Liberia, a country independent in theory but actually managed not by America but by the Firestone Rubber Company. It was governed for many years by a 'dictator,' who once told Gold Coast politicians who visited the place in 1952 or thereabouts that he, the dictator, did not fake the elections. There was no need, he said, but if there were a need, well, naturally he would fake them. These same Gold Coast politicians also remarked on their return, "Oh, how their drains smelled – but they owned them." When the Gold Coast politicians were striving for Independence, that was what they wanted – efficiency of drains, schools, etc. were minor points compared to running their own show.

At last, after 12 interesting and enjoyable but hot days (and nights) we reached the Gold Coast. We docked at Sekondi, or more precisely Takoradi, the new port which had been opened by the Prince of Wales a few years earlier. The road to Accra in 1929 was poor, and so were the motor cars. We could train up to Kumasi and down to Accra the following day, but it was quicker to stay aboard and be landed in Accra, the capital of the Gold Coast. But Accra had no harbour. The ships used to lie about a mile off shore, outside the perpetual coastal surf, and we would be lowered into large canoes. The method was for four of us to sit in a 'mammy-chair', with just room enough for four, be hoisted up by a crane or derrick, swung out over the ship's side, then lowered into the canoes. This was all right in fine weather but if there was a large swell it was not such fun. Not only would one have to wait for several minutes crammed in the tiny mammy-chair, but once when the swell was bad we were swung out over the canoe and then, as the ship rolled, swung in again and out over the other side. Rather eerie! Once, only once, we were swinging so much that the derrick hoisted us up to the mast head till the rolling had diminished. Then we were taken to the shore, maybe a mile of paddling, by the muscular Ga (the people who lived in and around Accra) boatmen with their enormous biceps. Then, when within say 200 yards of the shore, the steersman would halt us and watch for a suitable incoming roller that would carry us up the beach. With passengers they took great care and I never heard of an accident, but with cargoes, many a load was tossed into the sea. Then, as we grounded, some of these powerful men would hold the boat, some take the luggage ashore, others carry the ladies on to dry land, and, if the shore was very wet, we men too were lightly lifted and landed ashore.

CHAPTER 2

First Tour:
July 1929 – October 1930

Ashore, we were met by the Secretary for Native Affairs, Hugh Thomas, whose widow celebrated her 100th birthday in 1994, and whose brother, Sir Shenton Thomas, was Governor of Singapore at the time of its capture by the Japanese. Thomas lined us up, six of us Oxford cadets, and opposite us a line of Africans. Each line was then asked to step a pace forward, and the Africans we found opposite to us were to be our servants or stewards. I was lucky. I was given Kwasi Tandoh, a countryman from Sefwi, south-west of Ashanti, and a real gem he turned out to be. 'Kwasi' meant 'born on a Sunday.' In Europe we say we have 'birthdays,' but actually we have birth dates, while the Ghanaian truly has birthdays. Tandoh was a name of the ruling family of Sefwi. I paid him £4 monthly, and this covered his food and all other expenses, except that I also provided his uniform and a pair of shorts and singlet maybe twice a year. His first act as my steward – can you guess? – was to ask for an assistant, and so I took on a small boy, Kofi (born on Friday), at the princely sum of 10s. a month, but ample for his few needs.

Kwasi made a wonderful servant; not once did I ever think of locking anything up, and I never lost anything in all the 12 years he was with me. When in 1940 I was 'called up', I let Kwasi return to his country and gave him my 12 bore gun as a thank you. Like most stewards, such things as 'off-days' did not arise. He would have long holidays when I went on leave to the UK.

People used to say that the Malay stewards were far better, but Kwasi was as good as I could wish. It never mattered at what time I wanted dinner, or for how many people – it would be ready in no time at all. Once, when a Provincial Commissioner came to dinner who enjoyed cigars, mine were found to be mouldy. Kwasi dusted them, placed them in the cool oven, and the result, amazingly, was quite excellent. Only once do I remember him being late – so I visited the kitchen. I think it was the only time in 28 years I did such a thing. There was Kwasi, quite drunk, stirring the casserole, being held up by two other stewards, one on each arm, yet the dinner was none the less good and perfectly served in due course. I should say that the standard practice in those days was for the kitchen to be a separate building from the bungalow. Adjoining the kitchen would be the washhouse for laundry, and alongside, or separate, two or three small cottages or rooms for the servants.

During our time in Accra, in July 1929, we were taught the significance of 'signing books.' The Governor, Chief Secretary, Chief Justice, and a few other senior officials had 'Visitors Books' at their front door, and we were expected to sign them. I noted that on moving to Accra in 1932, I signed the books of 25 people (officials and non-officials). I wonder if the custom still applies? Old-fashioned, certainly, but it had its uses: in my latter days as Chief Commissioner every day's signatures were typed out in my office and the list submitted to me – an advantage to me to know who was in the station and advantageous to them since it was the custom that only those who signed received invitations to the sherry parties, lunches and dinners. The book was also used for saying thank you after a dinner – signing the book was much easier than writing a thank you letter. During my final three weeks in Ashanti, many, many people signed my book, a courteous way of their saying, "Sorry you are leaving us."

While in Accra we were also taken out to Achimota, the brand new secondary school built on the lines of an English Public School – expensive, but well worth it, something of which the Gold Coast was rightly proud. I shall have more to say about this later. After these few days in the capital, we were despatched to our destinations, whether in the Gold Coast Colony, Ashanti, or the Northern Territories. I and some six or seven others went to Ashanti, where we stayed in a Rest House in Kumasi. After a few days we were summoned to the Residency (which was to be my final home in West Africa). There were few cars, so at midday we had to walk there 'for a drink', but clad in our best linen suits, which were very hot. In due course Sir John Maxwell, the Chief Commissioner, Ashanti, a large and very able Scot from the Scottish Borders, came in and greeted us. "I expect you are all thirsty and would like a drink." We heartily agreed and soon we heard the sounds of glasses in the pantry, but the beer was slow in appearing. Just when it seemed to be forthcoming, we heard a car coming up the drive, whereupon Sir John said: "That will be Mr Cadbury. He is teetotal. John, take away the drinks." John Maxwell was known for his meanness but this we felt, was a bit hard, as, with dry throats, we returned on foot to our lodgings.

I was posted to Fomena, within the Obuasi District. Obuasi was where the Ashanti Goldfields mines operated, producing gold from one of the world's richest seams. However, being situated in a quartz reef, it was difficult and expensive to extract the gold. The mine was continually expanding, and never more so than in the 1950s, when General Sir Edward Spears took command. He was not a miner but a tactician, who handled Nkrumah with great friendship and success. The growth was subsequently sustained through the cunning of Tiny Rowlands of Lonrho.

Fomena is some ten miles from Obuasi. It was the seat of Kobina Foli, Omanhene (King or Head Chief) of the Adansis, a large and powerful tribe. In 1896 the British had marched from Cape Coast with Major R. S. S. Baden-Powell in charge of the Scouts – not Boy Scouts, but the front line troops, and all Ashanti had been against the British 'invasion.' The action taken by the British was to stop the Ashanti mercilessly raiding the Fantis and other tribes along the Coast. On this occasion Kobina Foli stood out and let the British troops pass through unmolested.

I was quartered in a primitive Rest House on top of a small hill just outside the town (or large village). No other white men were within ten miles. Kobina Foli used to visit me frequently – sometimes giving me a chicken, often eggs and vegetables. He felt a responsibility for this strange young white person. Basically I had two tasks, first, to learn the local language, "Ashanti," one of the various dialects of Twi spoken over most of Ashanti and the Colony, and second, to visit all the villages in the area, checking on their sanitary arrangements to see that they had adequate pit latrines, and if they had not, to tell them to dig them and ensure that this was done. I also had to check their water supplies. One of the bad diseases in Ashanti was 'Guinea Worm,' caused by drinking stagnant water. A large worm, maybe several feet in length, would wander through the body and eventually exit near the ankle. It was both painful and incapacitating, causing much ill health with people having to sit at home, unable even to go out and collect firewood.

I stayed in Fomena several months but was never lonely. Kwasi and Kofi looked after me well. I had plenty of work to do, and every now and then

I would walk the ten miles or so to Obuasi, with Kwasi carrying my suitcase, and spend the week-end with the District Commissioner, Capt. J. R. Dickinson. He was a Lancashire man and, like so many of my senior officers, had fought in World War I and had been recruited to the Colonial Service in the early 1920s. He had no University degree but a mass of common sense. He was liked by all the Europeans and was very popular with the Africans. Just two stories about him. One Saturday morning, Dickinson was sitting in court as a magistrate, hearing the usual Saturday 'sanitary' cases, when everyone pleaded guilty and the penalty was a 5s. fine for 'rubbish' and a 10s. fine for 'mosquito larvae.' As usual, the 20 or so women all pleaded 'guilty' and Dickie was just about to fine them all the usual 5s., when he noticed a Fulani woman, fair skinned from Northern Nigeria and beyond, carrying not only the usual babe on her back, but also one in front. "Are those twins?" asked Dickie. When told they were, he said, "Well, I think you have done your duty to the country, I will not fine you." Then, wishing to be fair, he added, "Anyone else here had twins?" There was a long pause, then an aged crone, looking about 80 but probably 60 plus, put up her hand. "Have you had twins?" he asked. "No," she replied, "but if you let me off I'll try." Court dissolves in laughter.

The other story was a civil case. A girl was suing for money, her boy friend having left her. "How much are you claiming?" said Dickie. "Five pounds," she replied. "And how often did he sleep with you?" he asked. "Oh, about a thousand times," she answered. Dickie then tried to work this out. "Five times 240 – the number of pence in a pound – that's about one penny a time: very reasonable, judgment for the plaintiff." Then, again sitting in court next morning, he thought he recognised her. He asked the Sergeant. "Yes sir," he replied, "it is the same girl you saw yesterday. When she got home she made a terrible fuss, shouting and screaming and saying, 'Everyone knows I am 2p. 2p., but the D.C. says I am 1p. 1p'." After that Dickie just could not bring himself to punish her.

One time I was staying with Dickie, and in the evening was playing the bagpipes on his front lawn, I had not noticed (it being dark) that I was standing on a 'river' of the powerful black driver ants. One does not feel them till they bite. I felt nothing till I suppose a hundred or so were well up my legs – then bite, did they bite! I dropped the pipes and rushed into the house, throwing off all my clothes and, with the help of Kwasi and Kofi, the three of us eventually picked them all off me, but was it painful!

I went up to Kumasi for the St Andrew's Night dinner. It was the usual gathering of Scots, some 70 of us, many in the kilt and dancing reels. I piped in the Haggis.

In May 1930, after six months as Assistant District Commissioner in Obuasi District, I was posted to another District. This was to Sunyani in Western Ashanti, not as Assistant DC, but on my own as Acting DC. District Commissioners were continually moved from one station to another. Perhaps when I was Chief Commissioner I was as bad. I'm not sure. But such moves were not really inconvenient. It was not like moving house in the UK for two reasons. First, every bungalow had its basic heavy furniture – beds, tables, chairs, etc., and second, all – and I mean all – the packing was done by one's stewards, Kwasi and Kofi in my case. Transport was undertaken by a Government department, which really handled it well (and, of course, at no personal cost). Again and again I might be working in one station on a Wednesday, have Thursday motoring, moving to another station maybe 150 miles away, and be in the office on Friday – and expecting, when I went home at noon, to find Kwasi had cooked me a good lunch. In addition to moving house, I usually travelled extensively in my District. In one tour I moved 115 times, sleeping in no less than 80 different beds.

At Sunyani I was in charge of the District, some 2,000 square miles, and with some 20,000 population. I was in sole charge of the Magistrate's Court, the District Treasury, Roads, the Prison, and had a sort of supervisory interest over Public Health and the Police, both of whom were under the responsibility of their own senior officers 80 miles away. My staff consisted of two clerks, who also acted as interpreters, office messengers, a bailiff, and I also used prisoners when I needed them.

The principal Gold Coast roads were maintained by the Public Works Department. The other main roads were kept by the DC, and village roads by the Chiefs. The 80-mile road from Kumasi to Sunyani was PWD. for 50 miles, then became my responsibility. In 1930 I had no funds for this purpose, nor indeed for any of the 100 or so miles which it was my duty to maintain. But if I didn't maintain them, I would be in trouble from my superior officers. My job was to see that the gutters were kept clean in order to carry off the tropical rainstorms, and where the surface was mainly mud, to have gravel laid. The work was accordingly done communally, that is, I would ask or tell the Chief concerned to improve a certain stretch of road. If the village was small, and no one there likely to be able to read, I would send my Bailiff with my 'Message Stick', which was similar to the Linguist Stick of a Chief. The Linguist Stick was the emblem of office carried by spokesmen for a Chief. My Stick, not unlike a Drum Major's baton, was different in that it had a silver-plated crown, under it the badge of the Gold Coast (an elephant under a palm tree), and below that the inscription, "District Commissioner". On the arrival of the Bailiff, the Chief would then beat drum, and the villagers would turn out and do the job. If the Chief refused, or if the work was not done, I could by law fine the Chief up to £25, but I do not recollect ever having to do so.

In those days we were fortunate in not being pestered by the 'media.' The following is a trifle imaginary, but not far from the truth. The police would telephone me: a small riot in a village. I would go out to see what was happening and see them make an arrest. Next morning I would sit in Court and the accused would plead guilty. I would sentence him, say "£2 or a week in prison." Having no money, he would go to prison. The following morning, as I went to do my regular prison inspection, I would see him smiling and happy. The 'hard labour' was not really very hard. He had a different set of clothes, different food to eat, and was really very satisfied – and as like as not would try to salute me and say, "Morning, Sah." And then I might see him again up at my bungalow during the week – possibly weeding the road to my house, possibly watering the roses in the garden, possibly polishing the house furniture, which was Government property. The 'media' might not have approved, but it was a system that worked and worked well.

The prison, I might add, was unlike ones in the UK. In fact it was an old British army post built after the last Ashanti rising in 1900. It was well constructed, but with sloping, rather than vertical, walls both outside and in. One day I went to the prison and knocked. No answer. Then I heard footsteps behind me, turned, and saw the gaoler running up to the building. He ran up the outside wall, down the inside one, unlocked the door, and saluted me smartly. "All present and correct, sir." The custom was for prisoners to work in gangs of four, escorted by a warder carrying a loaded gun, but the cartridges in it were so ancient, it is more than doubtful whether, if fired, it would have killed any one other than the person firing it. Again in my wanders around, I might come across a gang of prisoners sitting under a tree, one of them holding the gun while the warder sat nearby smoking a cigarette. Maybe not a perfect system but, as I have said, it worked. No one ever escaped, and very rarely did anyone complain.

I had to travel as much as possible – but how? I tried a motor cycle but the roads were so bad that I found it useless. Once I bought a car in Kumasi and started on the 80-mile journey home to Sunyani, but after some 40 or 50 miles the foot brake packed up and I was left with a weak hand brake. I drove slowly, but as I entered my garage at a real crawl, the hand brake finally broke. I hit the garage wall and as we bounced back the front bumper fell off.

Two years later I had a similar incident en route to Nkoranza, 36 miles away. I had to travel fairly fast as Kwasi had failed to wake me in time and the Chief Commissioner was due in Nkoranza to present the Queen Mother with the Gold Coast Badge and Certificate of Honour. Nkoranza was naturally crowded. My brakes had packed up early on, but I knew the road well. It was hilly, but I changed gear on all down slopes, and I had no fear – till I arrived in Nkoranza township. The whole square was full of people. Luckily, with my horn blaring and in a low gear, I just managed to come to a halt without hitting any person or thing. Just one other car story. One day I was driving with a friend on a forest road, up a steep hill and while he was changing gear, the gear lever came away in his hand. I've never seen that happen before or since.

Back to Sunyani, 1930. My first tour. The court work was not very heavy, mostly criminal. Nearly everyone pleaded guilty, which shortened court sittings. Then the Treasury: the work was not very taxing except physically – for all the transactions were in coin. Paper notes were not accepted for fear of their destruction by white ants, termites. Coinage was practically all in two shilling pieces, the florin, done up in bags of £100 and three bags to a metal box, which I would take with me on my travels and which could be padlocked to my bed. Some of the wealthier Africans would bury the odd £100 under the mud floor of their compound and only they, and no one else, would know where it was buried.

I travelled a lot, and the method was usually by small lorry. I would sit in front with the driver; behind would be my clerk (also interpreter), my orderly (not for protection, but as evidence that it was the District Commissioner in the lorry), Kwasi and Kofi, and bath, tables, chairs, cook's box, china, cutlery, clothing, etc., etc. Quite a business! Well, not really, for all the packing was done by Kwasi, and I did not need to miss even an hour's work in the office. On trek my business was, as at Fomena, to inspect village water supplies and village latrines, and also to hold general discussions with the Chiefs and anyone else who wished to see me.

In the Sunyani area there were no cattle and no horses, thanks to the tsetse fly and the Trypanosomiasis, or sleeping sickness, it caused. There were a few sheep, but of poor quality as they mainly lived on the village street. It was the same with chickens. The reason was that, outside the village, the forest or jungle appeared, and the only grass might be a small patch kept for football. Consequently, there appeared to be a lack of protein in the area. However I learnt to my amazement that the main source of protein was snails. These bred in the forest profusely, and an area was only harvested every six or seven years. The snails were dried, placed on sticks, say 20 to a stick, 20 sticks to a bundle, and maybe 50 to 100 bundles were sent on a lorry to Kumasi. Thus, in addition to the villagers' own supply of protein, snails were a useful source of income. But the main source of their revenue was undoubtedly cocoa.

Ashanti's forest was full of cocoa. In 1930 it held a good price but it could be very unstable, varying from day to day. At one time it rose from 16 shillings a ton to 211 shillings in just two years. The Gold Coast produced something like one-third of the world's cocoa. A few years later cocoa was invaded by a virus, 'swollen shoot,' which decimated the crop, but in 1930 swollen shoot had not arrived. Cadburys were the principal buyer of cocoa, but Unilever and several continental firms were also buyers. Sometimes, on trek at Berekum, near Sunyani, I might witness the Cadbury agent actually purchasing the raw cocoa. He would be sitting in the village square under a large umbrella at a neat table with a white cloth, a glass, an unopened bottle of whisky and some Perrier water, all provided by the locals. Cocoa bags would be much in evidence, some on the ground, having been carried in from the 'bush' – a word applied to any land other than a road or village – by strong Northerners paid 1s. a day. The agent would ask how much cocoa had been brought in – answer, say, 15 tons. The agent would write a message; this would be taken by car, at speed, to Bechem, 40 miles away. Then a telegraph to Kumasi, then a cable to England – to London, Liverpool, or Bournville – and almost immediately a return message would come, and within a short period of perhaps three hours, the answer would be in Berekum: "selling price eight shillings and sixpence a load," which was 60 pounds. There was no quibbling; that was the price that day. Soon the 15 tons would be on their way to Kumasi, thence to Takoradi, and so to the UK.

Another of a District Commissioner's duties was to try and settle boundaries, that is those between Head Chief and Head Chief. Land was, to the Ashanti, as to many folk throughout the world, the most important physical possession. This was not just for its physical value; it also had a sanctity that was often closely related to the 'origin' of the tribe. And all were prepared to go to extreme lengths to win their cases. The lengthiest and most expensive case was in the Colony, not Ashanti. It was in a cocoa area where a Sub-Chief considered he owned the land, whereas this was vigorously disputed by the Head Chief, the Omanhene of Akim Abuakwa, with the latter winning. His costs were £120,000, while the Sub-Chief's expenses totalled twice that – a lot of money in the 1930s, when a labourer's wages were 1s. a day.

In the Sunyani district many boundaries were known and also many were uncertain. One in particular was between two Head Chiefs, and I thought I would have a shot at this. How naive, almost stupid, I was! The problem had been slightly tackled by many of my predecessors, but then abruptly dropped. I went to see the two Omanhenes. The one, of British Gyaman, was in the north-west, in scrub or savannah land: poor and containing neither cocoa nor mahogany trees. The other, Berekum, lay west of Sunyani, in the forest: wealthy, with masses of cocoa and forest trees, then selling at huge figures. Both Chiefs were willing to meet with me. I insisted on no more than five followers each – or I knew talk would be impossible. The day before the meeting I slept in a delightful Rest House in Gyaman country – wide open spaces – but was I dismayed, as I was having breakfast, to watch steady streams of Gyamans following various paths, all leading to my rendezvous, and each carrying his usual farming implement, the machete, a very powerful weapon!

At the appointed time I duly arrived, accompanied by my Registrar (clerk and interpreter) plus one policeman, my orderly. After maybe half an hour, we heard sounds of the Berekums arriving – actually in ten vehicles, each carrying 20 able-bodied men and each of them with a shotgun. Now, most probably, all District Commissioners say 'Durbars'. It is an Indian word, but we misused it and referred to any large ceremonial occasion as a Durbar, but probably always one between friendly or reasonably friendly parties. This was different. There was total antipathy, hatred. The Head Chiefs had never met one another, nor did they want to. The 'greetings' were fantastic but just as described in anthropological textbooks. Gyaman would send a messenger to the 'invaders.' " Who are you? Why do you come? What do you want?" etc., etc. And each time an answer would come back, each time delivered in great pomp and style. Once this was all done – and the atmosphere was tense to say the least – water was sent for the visitor to wash his feet, his hands . . . "Was any food required?" . . . and so on it went for fully 30 or 40 minutes. At last the Berekums were admitted to the circle and I was asked to speak. All I could do was apologise, say I had asked for no more than five a side, admit it was now a fiasco, better all go home and I would try again. Then the ceremonies started again, but thankfully in peace. The Berekums left in their lorries, letting off their guns as they departed. Had there been a riot, and maybe several killed, I think I would (rightly) have been blamed, but I learnt a lesson. I returned to the Rest House – and beer had never tasted so good.

My first tour, in theory 18 months, was 15 months. During each tour we were entitled to 'local leave' of three weeks, but in practice it seldom happened. I had it once, I think, in my 28 years. But I had no complaint for after my 15 months I had a delightful trip home, leaving Takoradi on 16th October 1930 by Elder Dempster's *Apapa*, and then enjoying 15 weeks at home – mostly in Scotland, mainly in the Highlands, climbing 'Munros' (hills over 3,000 feet).

CHAPTER 3

Second Tour:
February 1931 – December 1932

I departed from Liverpool on 11th February 1931, on the *Apapa*. I was posted back to Ashanti, but this time to Kintampo. This was a delightful place in north-west Ashanti, in savannah country, that is, no forest and therefore not much wealth, but no starvation and no unhappiness. The Chief, Sarikin Fanyinamah, was exceptionally interesting. He was a Wangara, from a long, long way beyond the north-west of Ashanti. In his early life he was a slave trader, dealing with hundreds of captives. He may indeed have seemed very cruel to our eyes, but in those days life everywhere was cheaper. He served with the well-known slave trader, Samory. When the French took over the Ivory Coast, they chased him out. This was soon after 1900. He took refuge in the Gold Coast, in Kintampo, Ashanti. Here he was soon made Chief of the town – the only example in Ashanti of a non-Ashanti being made chief. His character altered with the surroundings. He proved to be an excellent ruler, accepted both by the British and by the local population. He became a good friend of mine.

One day Fanyinamah came to see me with a complaint that three women were being a nuisance in the town. I have a note in my diary that I then fined them, but a row developed outside my office, so I placed a dozen of them in the police cells for a couple of hours. Call it primitive justice – yes, it was, but it was also what was expected. Had I not acted promptly and decisively, I would have been considered a weak (and rather useless) District Commissioner.

Just as our manner of living in Britain has changed enormously in the last 30 or 40 years, so it has in Africa, certainly in the Gold Coast. Today in Ashanti, only the minority are illiterate, and Kumasi has a University with some 10,000 undergraduates. But in 1931 things were very different, and especially in Western Ashanti. Kintampo was easily the most backward part of Ashanti. But I enjoyed it! One trek I took was to Abease, a small tribe of 2,000 to 3,000 people, with no schools and no roads. It was hard work. One day I had to walk 24 miles, so started at 3 a.m. Abease was seldom visited. I think I only went there once. I took some 20 carriers for my luggage, also my clerk and two police orderlies. The luggage was more than usual because I took two demi-johns of drinking water, each of about five gallons. I did not expect to find any water fit to drink after I left Kintampo. 1931 was a census year and I had census officers posted throughout the District. On the whole they did well and the count was as accurate as might be expected, except in Abease. Here the officer I had appointed failed to take any action whatsoever, so I made the count myself at each village. They knew when I would be coming. All were ordered to stay till I arrived, which of course they did out of curiosity if for no other reason. I did the count in each village throughout the Division.

The local water supply was appalling, a ghastly round hole full of many years' accumulation of dirt, and never emptied, for it was sacred. But I told them to empty and clean it – a risky decision. I felt that, with 20 carriers and two police, they were not likely to cause an uproar but I was apprehensive. In many villages in the Gold Coast, the village maidens would be sent out to bring water for my bath, usually only a matter of a few hundred yards beyond the village. In Abease, however, they had to walk some three miles before they found water clean enough to satisfy Kwasi, even for my bath. The 'school' had maybe 10 to 15 children, taught by someone who had perhaps never been to school. This is no criticism of the Education Department; they were doing a splendid job in the towns and cities and gradually, but only so far as funds permitted, extending their work to rural areas. And I still remember the insects in my house! Kwasi had placed the table for my supper in the centre of the room and carelessly placed my Tilley lamp on it. When I came to dine, I had never seen so many and such a variety of insects in my life. I counted 150 insects of 20 different species, all on my dining table – and the table set for dinner.

So much for Abease. Now for Banda, a delightful Division out west, bordering with the French Ivory Coast. They have a language of their own. Here my first trek was one of three weeks and I covered some 200 miles on foot (for which we were paid 3p. a mile). It had to be on foot; there were no roads. It was delightful open country and it had quite a good Government Rest House. In the evenings I would walk out to the low lying hills where baboons abounded and they came near to see not me, but my dog. Occasionally it was rather frightening. I carried a rifle but was glad I never had to use it. Here, as in so many places, tribal boundaries were not known but it was more than that: the boundary between the Gold Coast and the French Ivory Coast had never been definitively demarcated – a fact that was quite immaterial to the Bandas.

When on trek, I would stay in government Rest Houses or in village huts or, more likely, in grass huts which would be specially erected against my arrival. In this last case, three of them would be put up: one for my bed, a second for my 'office,' for sitting, eating, reading, meeting visitors, etc., and a third as kitchen, where Kwasi would cook my chicken for supper and bacon and eggs for breakfast.

In Kintampo we had an eccentric doctor. He was a specialist in sleeping sickness, a hard worker and beloved by the population. He took me down one evening to show me something. In a typical round hut, mud walls, thatch roof, there was a lunatic lightly chained to an upright pole in the centre (again a blessing, no media!). It was undoubtedly the right answer. To have certified him would have meant him being taken to the one and only Gold Coast asylum, in Accra 300 miles away, never to see or be seen by his relatives again. Now his relatives visited him twice daily, fed and cleaned him, and the doctor was sure this was the best treatment. I agreed, but he hoped it would not become widely known.

A few years later I was in charge of Wenchi District. Kintampo was part of it and was hit by the deadly scourge, Yellow Fever. No vaccine against it had yet been discovered and there was no known cure. The disease was transmitted, like malaria, by mosquitoes, but of another variety. It had first hit Tamale in the Northern Territories, where there were perhaps 50 Europeans, and some five or six had died. There was sheer panic in Tamale. Then it hit Kintampo and one soldier died. There were only some six or seven Europeans there, and to lose one – well, who would be next? Luckily, no one else succumbed, but no one entered or left Kintampo while the scare was on. As soon as it was permitted (an infected mosquito only keeps its infection for a few days), I went to visit Kintampo. All was back to normal again.

Back to 1931. After five very happy months in Kintampo, full of the wide open spaces that many of us had come to Africa to see, I was moved—'transferred' to Mampong, one of the best districts in Ashanti. It was in the luxurious forest or jungle, but with splendid savannah in the northern half of the District. After a month there, I handed over to the substantive District Commissioner and then had three interesting months working in the Chief Commissioner's Office in Kumasi. Instead of being on my own, I was now definitely a subordinate. In the three months I was there, I suspect that I learnt what we were in Africa for, that is, first, to keep the peace (for every Division, as we called a Head Chief's area, had its internal feuds); second, to advance "civilisation" in the form of roads, schools, health, etc. etc.; and third, but never to be forgotten, to train the people to 'govern' themselves.

After working in Kumasi I had a delightful rural spell, three months as 'Travelling Commissioner, Western Ashanti' – wandering about a largely unknown, unmapped area, with scarcely any roads and still with a few small herds of the forest elephant. My job was to report on this little known area. During my time there I once had a walk of 211 miles over 18 days, often doing 18–20 miles a day and then a day or more in a village with the Chiefs and Elders. I had 22 carriers with me to carry the loads of myself, my clerk, and Kwasi.

Then, right out of the blue, I had a summons to Accra – to be Private

Christiansborg Castle

Secretary and Aide-de-Camp to the Acting Governor, Mr Geoffrey Northcote. The practice was that substantive Governors brought their own Private Secretaries but when they went on leave, the Colonial Secretary acted as Governor and took on a PS from the ranks of District Commissioners. During my eight months with Mr Northcote, till the Governor returned, I thoroughly enjoyed this totally different life. I stayed in Government House, Christiansborg Castle. This was a magnificent building erected by the Portuguese in about 1623, then captured by the Danes, and then by the Swedes who altered and improved it. It became Government House in 1900, and by 1932 had been fully modernised and made most comfortable. Office work was not heavy. There was an adequate number of clerks and most of the work was handled in the Secretariat by the Colonial Secretary and a large staff. My job was largely decoding cables. Usually an easy code was used for cheapness and speed, and rarely a cypher, which was usually difficult to work out and 'secret.' Then there were the dinner parties. I would suggest names of guests and arrange seating plans, all subject to approval, of course. When Mr Northcote intended to go on trek, it would be my responsibility to make all (I mean all) arrangements: luggage, transport, accommodation, entertaining, wherever we went. It was a marvellous opportunity for seeing the country, not just Ashanti, but the whole Gold Coast, and of meeting officials and unofficials and important African chiefs.

The work, as I say, was not too heavy, and while others played golf and tennis (from 4 p.m. to 6 p.m. daily, for being near the equator, the sun set at a similar time the whole year round), I enjoyed riding. I had ridden occasionally in Scotland, and at Oxford had joined the territorial Gunners, camping with them at Tidworth and deriving great exhilaration from galloping into mock action, riding one horse and steering another. Polo was also a great thrill. Not quite the standard of Hurlingham, nor its cost. I think polo cost me £3 monthly – £1 subscription, £1 10s. for horse feed, and 10s. wages to the horse boy. Each horse had a full time stableman. Because most of the Gold Coast was subject to the tsetse fly, polo was played in the far north, in Tamale, but not in the Colony except in Accra, where the polo ground was within a short distance of the sea with the stables alongside, so that the sea breezes discouraged the presence of the tsetse fly.

Living at the Castle, I enjoyed considerable luxury. Remember, however,

West Africa was still technically 'The White Man's Grave'. There were scarcely any European ladies, so few dances. Certainly we had plenty of tennis, and in the towns, golf, but no theatres, cinemas, art galleries, or anything academic or intellectual. Going on trek was fun but rough. There was little electricity so reading was by Tilley lamp, and there were always hosts of insects. We slept under mosquito nets. But Government House was comfortable. I could be playing polo till I heard, from the Castle about half a mile away, the dressing bell (though I think it was probably in fact a dressing bugle). I would drop what I held, the horse boy would take my stick. There was a Government House car waiting, engine running, and I would go straight to the Castle where Kwasi was waiting to remove my riding boots. The bath had been run and when I came out, there was Kwasi with a towel, my dinner jacket and a clean shirt. He would wind my cummerbund round me and I would be upstairs in time to receive the first dinner guests.

Many, but not all, dinners were very formal. Not only did the table plan

Christiansborg Castle – Dining Room and Punkah

show where you sat, but also whom you took in to dinner. There were no fans, not even in Government House, but a full length punkah pulled while we were at dinner. Even on informal occasions dinner jackets were worn, but on formal occasions it was tail coats or, under Colonial Regulations, a short, very small but smart white jacket and, of course, medals. I remember once a magistrate, actually a retired Naval Commander, arrived on a formal occasion wearing a dinner jacket with medals. I asked if he had not read the invitation which stated 'Medals.' He said he was wearing his. I replied, perhaps rather naughtily, that 'Medals' implied full evening dress. So he rushed home to rectify his error, but found the house locked and his steward gone, with the result that I had to rearrange the table and we dined without him.

Now, for two tales of locusts. First, and I think it was in 1932, Accra was 'invaded,' not by millions, but by millions of millions of the creatures. The whole town was covered by them. Everything green was eaten. Bushes were not only lacking in greenery, but every branch was thick with scores of locusts. Somehow or other they were poisoned and swept into the drains. These were huge, well maintained concrete tropical drains, some four feet across and four feet deep. Now, instead of taking off the tropical rain storms, they were filled from end to end and bottom to top with dead locusts. Unless one has seen it, it is hard to visualize. The whole of Accra, with these millions of millions of dead locusts and nowhere to dispose of them, stank.

The only other time I encountered locusts was in February 1931, when they were on migration. I was motoring north, in Northern Ashanti, beyond the forest, when I spotted a large black cloud approaching. What was it? Soon I was to know: locusts. I estimated the solid swarm to extend from ground level up to five hundred or one thousand feet, and to extend, maybe, to five miles long by one mile wide. Again, millions of millions. One could not even make an estimate. The car windows had to be shut. This was, of course, before air conditioning, and we usually drove with the windows wide open. We had to proceed very slowly because we could not see ahead, or scarcely even make out the gutters at the side of the road. We were fearful of meeting another vehicle, except that it also would be crawling. Our headlights made no difference. Above us, below us, all around us, there were just millions of locusts. What a menace!

Writing of locusts reminds me of butterflies. Once, while motoring on some rural road, my progress was actually impeded by them. It was a very hot day, just after a heavy shower of rain, and the road was full of puddles. Each puddle was blue or yellow from the several hundred or thousand butterflies on it. As my car approached, they would rise up. My radiator became blocked so that the engine boiled. We had to stop, pull out the dead butterflies, let the engine cool, top up the radiator – and continue; but the same would happen after another two or three miles.

So, to return to Accra. I very much enjoyed my time with Acting Governor Mr Northcote, not only in 1932 but again in 1934. I was eight months at Government House. Although I preferred living in a District and administering it, my stay at Government House was very comfortable. The work was often hard, in fact very hard, and the hours were long, but there were many compensations: polo, swimming, golf, tennis, and every day snooker, chess, or just social gatherings. But all good things had to end.

At the end of November Mr Northcote ceased to act as Governor, and the newly appointed Governor, Sir Shenton Thomas, arrived. He was later to be Governor of Singapore at the time of its collapse to the Japanese. Sir Shenton came with an Aide-de-Camp but no Private Secretary, which hitherto had been the custom. Acting Governors, as I have said, took a District Commissioner like me to do both jobs, but substantive Governors normally brought out their own Private Secretary and also a soldier to be ADC Sir Shenton's ADC was a soldier and a brilliant polo player, who, remarkably, played left-handed – a very rare event in polo and normally forbidden. Lotinga, the ADC, had had permission to play from, I suppose, Ranelagh or Hurlingham. When I tried to hand over to Lotinga the keys of the safe and the 'secret' and 'very secret' cyphers it contained, he refused. I had to hand over to Sir Shenton personally. As he took them, all he said was, "Blast Lottie!"

I sailed for home a few days later, on 11th December, and arrived in Edinburgh at midnight, 23rd December, in nice time for Christmas. I was met by both parents, my sister, and three brothers. Apparently, living in 'The White Man's Grave' was still considered quite an adventure by them.

After a full five months' leave, considered curiously long by so many in the UK who were accustomed to a mere four or five weeks holiday, I again took the night train from Edinburgh – the great Caledonian Railway – to Liverpool, breakfasted at the Adelphi, and sailed that afternoon on Elder

Dempster's *Apapa*. In Madeira I took a taxi up to no less a height than 4,400 feet, the same as Ben Nevis, and bought a few bottles of Madeira wine at the same 6s. a bottle – again, no inflation. Having spent much time while on leave taking bagpipe lessons, I had many hours on the poop enjoying myself practising.

I think it was on this voyage, late one night after playing bridge, and being bored, a companion and I (he had been posted to the Nigeria Regiment) saw a trap door while wandering about the stern of the ship. We lifted it and descended, level after level. We found ourselves going down to the depth of the ship. We had no idea where we were till suddenly we met the propeller shaft, something I have never seen before or since: this enormous shaft, steadily revolving and driving our ship forwards. Rather nervously, but we were young and not easily frightened, we walked forward, holding tight to a handrail, the propeller shaft only a couple of feet from our own feet. Suddenly we found ourselves in the engine room. Although we were in the usual evening dress, the oiler showed no surprise. He talked to us, then showed us how to emerge – up many, many flights of stairs. And so, back on deck once more, having been to the depths, we decided to go to the other extreme – and ascended the mast. Good steps, and as far as I remember, enclosed, so if we fell, we were not likely to fall far. We must have been seen from the bridge but no one took any notice, and when we bumped our heads on the trap door, the night-watchman opened it for us, and we climbed in to join him in the Crow's Nest. We had a chat with him ere descending, and this time we did go off to bed.

CHAPTER 4

Third Tour:
June 1933 – December 1934

We arrived at Takoradi at 5 a.m. on the appointed day, unloading our cargo but not the Accra passengers. Roads and vehicles were still too bad, so we continued on to Accra by the *Apapa*. We reached there in the late evening, stayed on board till next morning, and it was about 9 a.m. ere the surf boats took us ashore.

I had expected (and hoped for) an Ashanti posting again, but it was not to be. I was to spend the next year in the Cape Coast area prior to another spell at Government House in Accra. I had my office in Cape Coast Castle, a large British Fort built in 1662, which housed not only the District Commissioner and staff, but also the magistrate and court and prison. Cape Coast had a pleasant climate, as there was a sea breeze almost the whole year, daily from 10 a.m. till about 8 p.m. From there I moved to Winneba, a delightful residential area, with a club and a small 9-hole golf course. My days passed as usual, except that whether at Winneba or nearby Swedru, I spent many days in Court. Most cases were petty crime, the offenders pleading guilty. I still remember one day when the police were 'trying me out.' The details I cannot vouch for, but the following is not far off the truth. The normal trucks or 'mammy wagons', as they were known, were licensed to carry 20 passengers. One day, first case, wagon carrying 22, that is, two in excess. I fined the driver 5*s*. Next case, four in excess, fine 10*s*. Next, six in excess, fine £1. Next, eight in excess, £2. Next, ten, fine £5. Next 12, fine £10. Next, fifteen excess, fine £15. I was wondering how far this was going to go. Luckily there was only one more case, 20 in excess, or carrying 40 in all. I had no alternative but to send him to prison. Had we begun at the other end, the 20 over, he might have got off much lighter but remember, this was 1933, and we had no such things as 'Guidelines' for magistrates. These, I think, only recently came into vogue in the UK.

Another common offence in Swedru, as in many other places, was 'illicit

Cape Coast Castle

spirit.' In the Highlands of Scotland illicit stills seem to have been formi-
dable structures hidden in deep recesses of the glens, but in the Gold Coast
anyone could put one in his house. All that was needed was a length of
copper piping, which explained why many a motorist, leaving his car
unprotected, might not be able to start it. When he looked, he would find
the copper pipe leading from petrol tank to engine to be missing! And, of
course, no one would tell. Potable spirit was made from many fruits or
vegetables. It was 100 per cent pure alcohol and really dangerous to drink.
It was also occasionally used instead of petrol to drive motor cars or lorries.
It was so much cheaper than petrol, but harmful to the engine. The drivers,
in their mammy wagons, would bring in quantities of illegal spirit in the
4-gallon cans in which we bought our petrol. For carrying one tin, maybe
a fine of £1 and confiscation, for ten such tins (40 gallons – not uncommon),
maybe a fine of £25 and all tins and contents confiscated.

Whether here or in Ashanti, I would, I'm glad to say not often, have to
hear inquests. When I did, it was usually because a man had gone hunting

Elmina Castle

at night with an acetylene lamp on his forehead. Suddenly he would see a reflection, assume it to be an antelope, shoot, find it was another hunter, and the story we would hear in Court was: "I see meat" – whether antelope, monkey, cane rat – anything edible was called 'meat.' "I shoot, when I go there, I find he be my brother." I am glad to say this did not often happen, but I think most District Commissioners will have tried at least one such case.

Recreations at Winneba were delightful: a good golf course, tennis and the club, bridge there in the evenings, and swimming in a small pool filled with sea water at high tide. And as the bungalows were slightly isolated, I played my pipes often without receiving any complaints. I also enjoyed much bird watching in the open savannah, that is, grassland with quantities of shrubs. There was also a large lagoon. One could usually walk between the lagoon and the sea dry-shod – rainfall was not great and there was always high evaporation. But once a year, on a day fixed by the Paramount Chief, the 'bar' was cut, so allowing the waters of the large lagoon to escape into the sea. I went down to watch and recorded a gap which enlarged to about 100 yards, and I estimated that they were some 1,500 fishers catching all the fish trying to escape to the sea. Quite a spectacle.

Only one other note from Winneba. One day the Director of Geological Surveys happened to come into my office. I asked why the name 'Gold Coast'? He replied that it was truly named, that there was gold everywhere, not just at Obuasi and Tarkwa. It had been raining heavily and the town drains were full. He went outside, collected a pailful of water, panned it, and produced gold! It was only a minute quantity, quite uneconomic, but proof that there was indeed gold everywhere, and that the country had been rightly named the Gold Coast.

My next station was Cape Coast again, where I stayed for some six months, partly in the Provincial Commissioner's Office, partly in the District Commissioner's. Work was much the same, that is, office most days and only occasionally on trek, but there were more Europeans there than at Winneba and the club was better patronised. The club was 'European' but this was not in its constitution. Africans would have been welcome but 'club life' was new to them and frankly, few would have enjoyed it. In the club, in addition to bridge, I played much chess and snooker. We would work in the office till 4 p.m., have time for an hour's golf or tennis, then to the club, perhaps stay there till 8 p.m. or later, and drive home, where our faithful cooks would give us an excellent dinner at 9 p.m. or whatever hour we arrived.

At school I was keen on the Officers Training Corps, where I obtained a Certificate 'A.' At Oxford I joined the Gunners, mainly, I admit, for the free horse-riding, and there I obtained my Certificate 'B'. So it was natural on arrival in the Gold Coast that I should join the Gold Coast Defence Force. In 1930 I received my Commission from the Governor, and later from the King, as a Second-Lieutenant, so it is not surprising that in due course I was awarded the 'ED.', letters few understand. They are short for 'Efficiency Decoration,' which is the Colonial Service equivalent of the much better known 'T.D.', 'Territorial Decoration.' The Defence Force was merely a reserve of officers, and I also joined the Gold Coast Terri-torials. They had a Company at Elmina, just eight miles west of Cape Coast. We are now in 1933 and taking the Territorials seriously, and indeed, when not playing golf or tennis, I would be over in Elmina maybe twice or even three times weekly for lectures, parades or on the rifle range. There were also weekend camps.

Unlike Ashanti, Cape Coast was much more 'advanced.' Indeed, it had an élite of educated Africans, lawyers and doctors but not, alas, engineers, agriculturalists, etc. I was often in their houses, drinking or eating – and they, of course, equally fed with me. There were many people of mixed blood in Cape Coast, and this was largely a legacy of the days of the slave trade. I also attended the large Wesleyan Church in Cape Coast, where services were held in English. Presbyterian services were held in the vernacular, of which I did not have a large knowledge. Roman Catholic services were in Latin and the Anglican Church on the Gold Coast was 'high' – indeed, as regards incense, ritual, etc., higher than Rome! Anyhow, I was happy in the Methodist Church. But one day I happened to mention to the Rev. Gaddiel Acquah, the minister, who was well known to me, that Brodie Cruickshank, merchant in Cape Coast and later Acting Governor in 1853, had been a distant relative of mine. He was actually a cousin of my grandmother, so no true relation. During the course of the service, Gaddiel Acquah calmly announced, "And we are very glad to have worshipping with us today the District Commissioner, Mr Russell, who has ever so many relatives living with us in Cape Coast."

Before I leave Cape Coast, I would like to mention one real character we had. This was Dr Dyce-Sharp, who was knowledgeable on many subjects and a very popular but domineering man. The picture I like to remember of him is on the deck of a torpedoed and sinking Elder Dempster ship. When all had taken to the boats, Dyce-Sharp stayed on the bridge with the Captain and as the Captain went down with his ship, so did Dyce-Sharp. Two brave men!

Then, at the end of May I was recalled to Government House in Accra, again to be Private Secretary and ADC to Acting Governor Geoffrey Northcote. I really enjoyed playing polo. Indeed I played three times a week, and usually three chukkas each time. In the UK it is considered a rich man's game but not, as I have said, in Accra. Think of it: polo thrice weekly for £3 monthly! The pony I bought, 'Why Not,' cost me £13.

Shortly after my arrival, the Acting Governor, as was customary, put on a garden party for some 300 guests. My diary records my being very tired after it, the more so when the next Sunday I had to spend three or four hours on cables and cyphers, a tiring and uninteresting 'game.' So it is not surprising that soon after that I went to hospital for a few days. I think, basically, it was just malaria, as the quinine which I took daily was not totally effective. However, a fortnight later we all went on trek for 21 days. I shudder to think what plans I must have made. Where would we sleep each night? Where would we entertain? For it was the practice of the Governor to take over the house of the Senior Officer in the station and do all the entertaining. Where would we entrain? Where would we take to the motor cars? Times for each movement? When to wear uniforms, what time to dress, when and where to change back into mufti, etc.? We had to take most of the food with us and all the drink. All this had to be done well in advance, and a programme had to be printed and distributed for all concerned – maybe 100 copies.

Just a few details of the start. We drove to Accra railway station in the evening, had dinner on the train in the Governor's private coach, slept, next morning off-loaded at Juaso, drove to the Konongo gold mine, then on to Agogo for tea and Kumasi for the night. Next morning a Palaver, in uniform, but golf in the afternoon. Next day the train at 8 a.m. to Akrokerri, formal meeting with the Head Chief, then down to Obuasi to see the gold mine and meet the mine manager, and then back to Akrokerri and dinner and sleep in the train. Next morning, train to Tarkwa, then by car, and of course lorry for all the luggage, to Sefwi in the far west. Back again, and on the train to Sekondi and at last by car to Accra on the 29th – a 21-day trek. Today people often compliment me on my 'administration.' There is no doubt where I learnt it!

While the Castle was being re-furbished, I had lived in a bungalow in Accra, but in September 1934 I moved to the Castle and sold my car for £16. Very soon His Excellency himself went into hospital, but as a dinner party had been arranged for no less than 32, Mrs Northcote and I ran it ourselves, and successfully.

In November the Gold Coast was due to have a new Governor as Sir Shenton Thomas had been transferred elsewhere. This was to be Sir Arnold Hodson, shrewd and able but eccentric. Throughout the Colonial Empire we enjoyed considerable pomp and ceremony. It was admittedly a nuisance to put on uniform (sword, gorgettes, and so on), but the Africans loved it and their Head or Paramount Chiefs turned out with their gaily coloured umbrellas, masses of drums and horns, etc., etc. And I think such pomp and ceremony prevailed everywhere (till Chris Patton recently stopped it, as far as he was concerned, in Hong Kong). Our Colonial Secretary sent off to Sir Arnold the usual proposals for his landing – who he would meet, route to the Legislative Assembly, Guards of Honour, swearing of the Oath of Allegiance, etc., etc. – probably some four or five pages. We were surprised to receive in reply no comments on the proposals but, "Please put a camp bed in my bedroom," and "What do you pay a cook in Accra?" I acted as his Private Secretary for about three weeks and enjoyed it. He was a keen golfer, also an excellent rifle shot. He and I often played a few holes on 'the Beach Golf Course.' One used to think of a Governor as not elderly but at least mature, and so Sir Arnold was himself, but he had married the daughter of his best friend, from a well-known Aberdeen family. His wife was only in her early twenties and her brother was actually still at boarding school in England.

Sir Arnold was not mean but, rather like my first Chief Commissioner, Sir John Maxwell, very canny with the baubees. At a large dinner, after the ladies had left, the Governor saw a certain guest talking to one of the stewards. "Everything all right, Bamford?" he asked. Bamford was a Lt. Col. in charge of the Gold Coast Police and had a conspicuous war record, having been at Passchenchdaele and commanded a South African Battalion. His reply was worthy of him. "Yes sir, everything's all right. I am just asking the steward to bring a pair of scissors to cut the last cigar in two." Sir Arnold's claim to fame in the Gold Coast was his 'cable radio.' He had begun this in the Gambia and brought with him his technical adviser, and though we were all very suspicious of it, in Accra it worked well. Very few of us had our own radios, or wireless sets as we called them, and for 2s. a month cable radio was excellent.

After three weeks with Sir Arnold, it was time for leave and I sailed on 9th December on the M.V. *Accra*. There was nothing special until the end of my leave, when Britain was celebrating the Silver Jubilee of King George V. On Monday, 7th May, like many others, we were out viewing bonfires all over the south of Scotland. Then back to Edinburgh, and at midnight, several of us went up Arthur's Seat. By 1.30 a.m. I set off in my car for Liverpool. I was there by 8 a.m., handed over my car to the shipping line, took the 10 a.m. train back to Edinburgh and arrived at 3 p.m. on Tuesday afternoon. I spent the night in Edinburgh, left again at 8 the next morning, Liverpool by 2 p.m., and on board, including my motor car, by 3, soon to set sail. I think it is worth showing these times.

Trains were slow but reliable, and I seem to have had no qualms in leaving Edinburgh in the morning in order to be on board ship the same afternoon in Liverpool.

CHAPTER 5

Fourth Tour:
May 1935 – January 1937

My next tour began in May 1935. My diaries were still written in pencil, and are difficult to read. I suppose 'biros' had not yet been invented. It was to be a dull tour – all in the central belt of the Colony, but with no less than ten moves. There is no doubt why, having moved house so often in the Gold Coast, I have never been appalled at doing so in Scotland. But more seriously, never being in any one station for long in this period, I never felt it was 'my District,' but only that I was holding the fort for another while he was on leave.

I noted that I was still paying my 'boys' what I had done six years earlier, that is, there was still no inflation. Kwasi was receiving £4 monthly, but temporarily reduced to £3 10s. for being hopelessly drunk one evening. It was a very rare occurrence, although he drank quite a fair quantity of the local tipple, palm wine. I paid Dubbie Moshie, from a tribe towards Timbuktu, £3 monthly.

When I was not suffering from malaria or some kindred illness, I was young and strong. Once, while on a fortnight's Territorial training with the Gold Coast Regiment in Kumasi, I recorded a 15-mile route march in the morning and 12 holes of golf in the afternoon. I think we must have been more 'war conscious' than parts of Britain, for I was made to take my Territorial training seriously, and apart from these two weeks in Kumasi, I was still regularly going to Elmina for parades or lectures and even to a five-day camp there.

On 25th May I was in Cape Coast. We had our usual Empire Day parade. It was, in fact, very formal, for we paraded in uniform with sword, gorgettes, and the rest. Then, in the afternoon the usual 'sports' in which everyone took part. It was on this day that some of our office clerks approached the Provincial Commissioner and asked, "Could we have a race just for gentlemen?" They were asked to retire and consider how to define 'gentlemen.'

The reply they gave was, "one who had not been to prison." Sports finished at 4 p.m. I had time for 18 holes of golf and snooker at the Club in the evening – a full but not uninteresting day.

I did not have as much 'trekking' as in Ashanti but was far from stationary. Let me mention Twifu, a ghastly small station I had to visit. I daresay it is spotless today, but it was not in my time. I am not likely to forget my first night there. I had my tin bath with me but did not need to use it for, to my surprise, in the dilapidated Rest House there was actually a bath. Dubbie filled the bath as usual and I proceeded to bathe. And then, as is customary, I pulled the plug, got out, and started to dry myself, but looking around realised that the bath was not connected to any pipe. The water was just running across the mud floor and out through a hole in the (mud) wall. And worse was to come, for the driver ants were on the prowl. This was unusual. They had to feed, but though I saw these large driver black ants often, indeed very often, they were nearly always on the march and easily avoided. I mentioned before how at Obuasi, while playing the pipes, I was caught and painfully bitten. Well, here they had invaded the Rest House. I managed to get into my camp bed, and Kwasi, very bravely, came and tucked my mosquito net in really firmly, so that no ant could actually get into the bed. I slept, even if not soundly.

When the morning came, I noticed a curious thing hanging in the open window. As was customary, the local chief had given me a present on arrival. This was usually a sheep or a chicken, a yam, and masses of eggs (these eggs did the rounds and were rarely fresh). This time it had been a lamb and Kwasi, having cut it up, hung a leg for safety in the window. The ants had found it, however, and if, say, 10 inches across, it was now 12 inches across. A string which held it appeared to be composed solidly of ants, an inch in diameter. But they had also made their own 'ant string,' filling the gap of say 12 inches between the leg and the lower window sill. Alas, the meat was so infected that it had to be thrown away.

Twifu was on the railway, only a side line with only two trains a day, but good for carrying cocoa in season. I was once travelling along the line in a small two-seater, being manhandled by two strong men, and I stopped to speak to some linesmen. They told me that 'wedges' holding the line to the sleepers loosened after every train passed, and their job was to walk the line daily and tighten them.

On one of my transfers to Winneba, which, I have said, was a delightful station on the sea, my first task was, as usual, to drop 'cards' on the senior local people – medical, police, heads of firms, and so on. It was the custom, and had many good points in its favour, but I remember the Director of Geological Survey (who dealt almost entirely with rocks millions of years old) calling my conduct 'pre-Cambrian.'

I was in Cape Coast for Christmas, normally a family affair, but we did our best and had a tremendous curry for 35 or 40 of us at the club. And so another tour ended, and I sailed from Takoradi on the *Abosso* on 25th January 1937. Instead of going on to Liverpool, I disembarked at Plymouth, managed to reach London that day and be in Edinburgh the following morning for breakfast.

After an enjoyable five months' leave and a much needed rest (for though usually fit, I did suffer from malaria, etc. too often), my parents took me out to Romano Bridge one Tuesday evening. It was one of their favourite resorts. On our return, I left Edinburgh at 11.30 p.m. and drove through the night to Liverpool. I arranged for my car to be put on board, and also a dog I was taking out, a Staffordshire bull terrier. In due course I boarded the ship, the *Adda*, and sailed at 3 p.m. on Wednesday.

CHAPTER 6

Fifth Tour:
June 1937 – October 1938

On this tour I was to have six months in Cape Coast and then back to Ashanti. In Cape Coast my diary usually just records "o.a.u." – office as usual. That is what it was: work, and really rather dull. Now and again we did have 'riots' in towns. Most of the coastal towns had disputes which occasionally, but luckily rarely, degenerated into fighting. More often than not it was just a show of guns – a modern shotgun was a status symbol but the majority had muzzle-loading firearms, down which one rammed the gunpowder, then the bullet. The 'bullet' might be anything and was quite often a sparklet bulb of the sort we used in our soda water syphons. Once I had to rush out to Kommenda, where a riot had occurred. Luckily, there was no one dead, but some 30 wounded. Having seen that all was quiet again, and that some Government Police were left there, I happily returned to Cape Coast.

One of my piping friends in Cape Coast was Hastie-Smith, master at Adisadel, the excellent Anglican Secondary Boarding School. He later served with the Gold Coast Regiment in Burma, then was ordained, and after the war came back again to Adisadel, this time as chaplain. On retiring he was appointed priest of the Episcopal church in Forfar, and so was again my near neighbour.

In Cape Coast we worked hard even if it was rather dull. We were not idle, and unquestionably the 'social' life was not too bad. There was golf and tennis, and I had much rifle shooting with the Defence Force as well as lectures and parades; then, in the evenings, to the club for bridge, chess, or snooker, and piping at home. Really, it was not too bad a life. My social activities included a number of drinks parties or dinners with the leading Africans. One of these was Arku (later Sir Arku) Korsah, then a solicitor but later to become Chief Justice. Another was Ward Brew, senior member of the Gold Coast Bar. Kobina Sekyi I met occasionally, but he did not 'fraternise,' for from early on he was always anti-white and longing for 'self-rule.'

I remember one day – it was somewhere around this time – when my Chief Clerk said to me: "Sir, I have divorced my wives and married a Christian one." His former wives, maybe two or three, were probably Christian, but he meant that he had previously been married under Native Customary Law and now he had married under Statutory Law, under which, as in the UK, marriage was monogamous. The differences in his habits were considerable. Formerly he would precede his wife walking to church and they would sit apart; at meals, she would serve him and not eat herself until he had finished; and she would wear the customary women's clothes. Now he would walk with his wife to church and they would sit together; at meals, they would eat together; and she would normally wear a blouse and skirt. But this kind of 'progress,' if so we may call it, was part of the gradual change from matrilineal to patrilineal succession (as we have in the western world). In Ashanti a boy was the responsibility not of his father, but of his mother's brother, and a man would be inherited not by his sons but by his sister's children. All this, however, is rapidly changing, especially in urban areas.

I had another ten days in hospital, in Accra, attended by the excellent Dr A. A. Gillespie who, like me, entered the Ministry of the Church of Scotland on retirement and was ordained to a parish near Peebles. On coming out of hospital, I was given three days before resuming work, so I drove west, beyond Sekondi to Axim, where my cousin, also Arthur C. Russell, was in charge of the Forestry Department there.

One of our tasks or duties was to give permits to chiefs to buy gunpowder. This was then issued to his people, mainly for ceremonies which always included quantities of gunfire and also libations. Drunkenness was rare, though vast quantities of gin, usually Dutch 'Schnapps,' were consumed. As more and more people bought modern double-barrelled shotguns, they had to come and get a permit to buy cartridges. I noted one hunter who requested the usual 200 cartridges. I asked him what he had killed with the last 200 and he told me, truthfully or not, "100 monkeys, 40 birds, and about 30 other miscellaneous." Not many shots wasted!

It was 1938 and I noted in my diary, 'Airmail available,' but I doubt if it was then reliable. In January I was posted back to Ashanti, first to the Chief Commissioner's Office and then as Acting District Commissioner,

Kumasi, the daily market

Kumasi. This I enjoyed. I remember one day a senior Kumasi chief coming into my office. I should say something about the Chiefly system in Ashanti. After the British invasion of Ashanti in 1896, Prempeh, the Asantehene or King of Ashanti, had been deported first to Sierra Leone and then to the Seychelles. He was allowed to return in 1924, but only as a private citizen. In 1935, his successor, Prempeh II, was recognised as Asantehene once more. We assumed, rightly, that the Ashanti were no longer interested in war against the Fanti of Cape Coast or other peoples of southern Ghana. There were five senior Paramount, or Head, Chiefs and many lesser ones, scattered throughout Ashanti. In addition, Kumasi itself had huge Clans with many – I could almost say innumerable – sub-chiefs. Some of these Clan Chiefs had rank equalling the five principal Paramount Chiefs.

One day one of these senior Kumasi chiefs, the Akyempemhene, came into my office, and asked for a plot of land in Kumasi where he wanted to build. I was very naive, and had not realised the implications or that he had been trying to obtain this plot from all my predecessors and had failed.

Kumasi Durbar, the Silver Drums

I at once gave it to him. (It was very similar to what I learnt, but only some 50 years later, when I was a Councillor on Angus District Council: that is, the value, sometimes the huge value, of having planning permission). The Akyempemhene was so delighted that he later sent a large ivory tusk up to my bungalow. Now under Colonial Regulations we were not allowed to accept gifts without permission, so I wrote asking permission to keep "a piece of ivory I had been given." Permission was granted, but when the Chief Commissioner was in my house not long after, he commented on such a large, fine piece of ivory. When I said he had given permission to accept it, he showed surprise. "I thought it was some small table napkin-ring or such like!" he said. He had, however, given permission, and I treasure this gift today. Also, under Colonial Regulations, there was a rule that when we did receive a gift or gifts, we were duty bound to return something equivalent or greater. Now it so happened that Prempeh II, the Asantehene, had just started a small six- or eight-hole golf course in Kumasi. He did himself sometimes play on the 'European' course around the Residency, but he also wanted his own course. At that time – or even today – I doubt if many chiefs played golf. The Asantehene was streets ahead of lesser breeds. Anyhow, my friend the Akyempemhene also tried to play golf – atrociously it is true, but at least he tried. So, on my next leave, I bought a golf bag and five clubs which I brought out with me and I presented these to him. I thought, given the approximate value of the ivory tusk, that I had complied with Colonial Regulations. He, of course, was delighted.

Another recreation I enjoyed in Kumasi was playing hockey with the regiment, black and white together. It was not a game I had ever played before, but I enjoyed it, though I was probably glad that we seldom played 7-a-side. The regiment also had a squash court and, although Kumasi was far too hot for such a game, many of us played it – but not very many games, I assure you. I was made an honorary member of the mess, and this I took advantage of, not only for the hockey and squash as I have said, but I often dined there on guest nights in full dress, as the British Army did until World War II and perhaps still does.

In Kumasi there was another African whose company many of us enjoyed. This was C. E. W. Bannerman, the first black African to become judge of the Supreme Court of the Gold Coast. And he was, indeed, very black and proud of it, but he boasted of his one-sixteenth Scots blood. He used to invite a few DCs to lunch. It was always curry, and each time we were amazed at the quantities of red pepper he could swallow. Any European would have been perspiring, even ill, with a tiny fraction of what he ate.

In March 1938 the Governor arrived in Kumasi for a splendid Durbar with twin objects. The Asantehene was to be decorated with the insignia of the order of Knighthood, the KBE, and the Gold Coast Regiment to be presented with a set of Silver Drums, given by the people of the Gold Coast. I was proud to have been at that ceremony, and still more so when on my final retirement in 1957, the Silver Drums were paraded and played at the railway station on my departure. The Durbar was a magnificent spectacle. Many Political Officers were in their white uniforms. Crowds of chiefs came from throughout Ashanti, each with their magnificent enormous umbrellas, and numerous drummers and horn blowers. Try and imagine the noise! I, as District Commissioner, Kumasi, had to lead, and to introduce His Excellency to, the various Kumasi chiefs, including the Asantehene. I think I am right in saying that near to the Asantehene was the Golden Stool, the heart of Ashanti and the cause of the 1900 uprising when the Governor was believed to have asked, "Why have you not produced your Golden Stool and let me sit on it?" For no one sits on the Golden Stool and indeed it has its own entourage, more sacred and important even than that for the Asantehene himself. It is paraded about once in every three or four years, so it was a great thrill to view it on this day, though from several yards away. No one other than its sacred bearers is allowed near it.

I had been posted to Kumasi in January, but it is not until 29th May that my diary records, "dined alone." As I say, we worked hard and also played hard, both physically and socially. There were only a few white women there in 1938, so dances were rare but, as I have mentioned, there was plenty of bridge, chess, snooker, and just social gatherings.

In August I had a day's hunting, seeking antelope. I had hired a hunter for the day. We were in savannah, not forest country. My diary records that we saw three waterbucks and tracks of hartebeest, bush cow (buffalo), warthog, and a few others – but only their tracks. The Gold Coast had a few elephants, a few lions, a few leopards, but in total very little 'game' other than the smaller antelopes. These were called duiker, and there were five or six sorts of them. I sent quite a variety of them to the Edinburgh Zoo. But I rarely went hunting. Indeed, in all my time, though I shot many green pigeons and bush fowl (akin to a partridge) for the pot, I killed but two antelope, one a roan and the other a hartebeest whose horns I still have. I did spend a number of days in dense forest seeking the most elusive bongo: I not only never shot one, but never even saw one.

Again, I spent ten days in hospital. I imagine it was malaria, but when I came out I was, as usual, fit and ready for hockey, squash, etc. One day I had a dinner party for eight, of whom five were black, including two African judges. This would become common in the 1950s but was unusual in the thirties. Shortly after this I spent a week doing an officers' course, and feeding in the mess. Hard work again, but different and enjoyable.

Soon after my return to Kumasi, my first cousin A. C. Russell wrote to me. He was not, as I have mentioned, a DC, but was in the Forestry Department. Like most of the Gold Coast Forestry Officers, he had studied Forestry in Edinburgh University. He was getting married and I was to be his best man. Unfortunately the bride's father failed to accompany her to the Gold Coast, so I was invited to give her away in his place, and a great honour and pleasure this proved to be. The wedding was in Sekondi, in the Roman Catholic Church, and the officiating priest was Swiss, with little of the English language. The bride was Jean Tullis, and the priest caused much amusement when he addressed her as "John Tullie!" After the wedding I returned to Kumasi to finish my tour, just some ten days, and then returned to Sekondi/Takoradi. The two places are only a few miles apart, Sekondi being the civic, political, and trading centre, and Takoradi merely the port. Having earlier met Jean Tullis off the MV *Accra*, I myself then duly sailed home on it.

Twelve days later, early one morning, we again landed at Plymouth. I was met by my brother Douglas, who was then a master at Dartmouth, where I greatly enjoyed staying. I had visited Douglas there some 12 years previously, when he was a midshipman. I then went up to London the next day and took the usual night train to Edinburgh.

The opening of 1939 was busy. On 19th January I proposed to Elma Strachan. She accepted. I nipped down to London, and on 26th January (as mentioned earlier) was called to the Bar. Time was short as I was due to sail on 22nd February. On 28th January we announced the engagement, and were married on 18th February in St Giles Cathedral, Edinburgh, by our great friend – of both the Russells and Strachans – Dr Charles Warr. We had the reception and showed our presents at Pittendriech, the Strachan House, where Douglas Strachan had his studio. Then we rushed into town and took the train to Markinch for a two-day honeymoon at Alburne Knowe, which had been kindly vacated by my dear Aunt Madeline. On Monday we returned to Edinburgh and slept in my parents' house. On Tuesday we slept at the Strachan's Pittendriech, and, early on Wednesday, with many to see us off, caught the 9:20 a.m. train to Liverpool: that is Elma and I plus her trousseau and some nine large crates containing most of our wedding presents, so ably packed and brought to the station by Jenners of Edinburgh. We reached Liverpool by 3 p.m. and by 4, with all our luggage, we happily set sail on the *Accra*.

CHAPTER 7

Sixth Tour:
March 1939 – November 1940

Early in March we arrived at Takoradi and caught the train to Kumasi, where the Chief Commissioner kindly had us both to stay at the Residency. After a couple of days we were off to Wenchi, a station I already loved, and which Elma and I were to enjoy for nearly a year. It was a beautiful spot: a good house, large garden, some fine ornamental and fruit (guava and mango) trees, and extensive views in many directions of places 30 or more miles away. In season at night we would admire literally dozens of fires burning off the grass to encourage new growth and thus bring in more wild life – duiker and so forth.

Wenchi was an Ashanti chieftaincy, but in Wenchi town there was a large Zongo, a word indicating 'strangers.' In practice the strangers were all Northerners, usually from either the Timbuktu area, or Hausas and

Wenchi, DC's bungalow

Fulanis from Northern Nigeria. Their chiefs always had horses, stallions. I might mention that there were no mares in the Gold Coast, for the French Colonies that surrounded the Gold Coast did not allow them to be exported. So not only when I played polo in Accra were all the ponies stallions, but so were the ponies that the Zongo chiefs sent up for Elma and me to ride. And powerful ponies they were, but with cruel bits – ghastly jagged bits of metal. One had barely to touch the rein and the beast halted. When I say 'cruel,' I refer to the actual bit, not to its use, for the Zongo chiefs loved their horses and treated them well.

Luckily there was not much office work in Wenchi, but a lot of travelling which I enjoyed. On long journeys I would fill the petrol tank full and put in the boot a 44-gallon drum and two 8-gallon drums; that is, I would leave home with some 70 gallons, or over 300 litres, of petrol. Very soon after we arrived in Wenchi, Elma and I set off for a six-day trek, but this time on foot, to Banda. The practice was for Kwasi and a porter or two to start early. Then Elma and I would set out at, say, 7 a.m. After a mile or two we would come across Kwasi with bacon and eggs and coffee ready for us. How we would enjoy this! Banda was my favourite place, perhaps because there were hills near the town where I could go for walks and be accompanied by the baboons, who always came to have a look at me, or rather at my dog, which they would have liked to kill. Me they would not have touched. And then, as so often, on my return to Wenchi I had a temperature, usually around 103° (40°C approx), and so had a few days in bed, accompanied by large doses of quinine and whisky.

By now, perhaps because we were two in the house, I had increased the boys' monthly wages, though not by much: they were £4 5s. for Kwasi, £3 10s. for Dubbie, £1 for a new boy, Kofi, and the same for a gardener. Kofi proved to be a great acquisition for he learnt to drive my car. It was part of my job to pay the labourers. At this time the standard wage for roadmen was 1s. a day or 26s. per month. I paid them monthly and each labourer, about 150 of them, received his wages in florins. You can imagine the weight of coin I had to transport!

In olden times one of the sources of the wealth of Ashanti was kola, and when I was stationed at Wenchi, up to the war, I would see long streams of donkeys, maybe 30 or 40 at a time, carrying dried fish that had been caught on the River Niger near Timbuktu. They would go no further, as they did not want to risk the tsetse fly killing their donkeys, so they would

load up with kola nuts in Wenchi and depart back to the north. After the
war there were no more donkeys – the trade had been motorised.

Unlike parts of the Gold Coast Colony, there were few inter-tribal or
inter-family disputes in Ashanti. In fact we were able to concentrate on
developing farming, commerce, trading, and some, although not much,
kola and ground nuts production. And we could get on with building schools
and making roads. My work was, basically, to encourage 'local government.'
Of the six or seven areas under Head Chiefs in my District, I decided to
concentrate on Nkoranza. I tried to persuade the people to initiate some
form of tax. I began by persuading the Head Chief to tax adult males, each
to pay 1s. per annum. It does not sound much, but it was several years
before the system finally worked and could be applied in other areas. At
this time all rule was by the Chiefs and their Elders – 'Elders' referring to
Linguists (spokesmen), Chiefs, and sub-Chiefs. My job was to encourage
the Head Chiefs to appoint 'young men,' a term that means anyone other
than a Chief, to their Councils and to their Native Courts. The Native
Court had large powers in customary law and in land cases, but only limited
jurisdiction in criminal matters. In fact the criminal side of the court was
'codified' in accordance with government laws. We thus had two sets of
laws running parallel. Strange to say, the system worked, but it was not

Bamboi Ferry

easy and the Government was soon to create the post of Judicial Adviser. I, with my legal qualifications, was one of the first to be so appointed.

Elma and I used to enjoy our rides in the evenings and also we were delighted to have Arthur Russell and his bride to stay with us. Having had many cars, all cheap and most of them barely doing their job, we bought a new van, actually a small Ford lorry, for £200 and had a cab or roof built over the driver, so that Elma and I could sit there without being too sunburnt. One bank holiday weekend Elma and I decided to make a camp at a place miles from anywhere. We drove to Bamboi on the River Volta, the boundary between Ashanti and the Northern Territories, and also between me and the DC in Bole. At Bamboi we hired a canoe and were paddled upstream for several miles till we were far away from the nearest human beings. We were put ashore, and after the boys had helped to set up our tents, they left. Elma and I had three delightful days there on our own, doing our own cooking, fetching our own bath water, etc. We did not dare bathe in the river. There were too many crocodiles and also many Gold Coast rivers, especially the slower moving ones, were carriers of bilharzia, a very nasty disease.

War was soon to break out but my diary records little of it. I did note in my diary, however, that on 24th August a telegram was received telling me not to go on trek. Otherwise life went on as usual, and this order must have been withdrawn. Even on 3rd September I do not mention the declaration of war. My diary only recorded personal events, not even my work, but a few days later Elma and I were undertaking a survey of the road to Bedu. It was not really a road, but a twisty path through thick jungle. Elma would go in front as far as I could still see her. I would then take a compass bearing and pace the distance to where she had been. Meanwhile she had gone on again – and so the exercise would be repeated. It was a slow business. Maybe we would survey two miles a day, and took about four days for the nine miles. I then plotted our work, calculated the angle start to finish (the village), and persuaded the villagers to cut this new line. Maybe thanks to some luck, we did arrive bang in the village, and had reduced the distance from nine miles on the twisty path to six miles on the intended road. The villagers were, of course, delighted.

I often mention malaria. Reader, do not think of this too seriously, for it was really more akin to influenza. For example, one day I had a temperature of 100° (38°C approx), the next day the same, but I drove the 50 miles to

Kintampo, worked and slept there, temperature 102°, and then returned to Wenchi. New drugs were beginning to appear. Quinine obviously did me little good, and I was now given atebrin. We'll see how it helped.

Elma and I spent the Christmas of 1939 in Kumasi, then had a few days in Accra. We returned to entertain the Chief Commissioner and his wife for the New Year in Wenchi. And, soon after, Elma being pregnant, I drove her down to Takoradi and saw her on board the *Apapa*. Many of those proceeding on leave at this time went to South Africa, but Elma was lucky – she got away to the UK (All Elder Dempster's boats, by the way, began with the letter 'A,' and were named after places in West Africa). I then motored back to Kumasi and was in Wenchi next day.

Still no mention of the War in my diary. In February 1940, actually while visiting Sampa on the western frontier of my district, I crossed over the international boundary to Bondoukou, a large French Ivory Coast town, and stayed the night there. But the French were still our allies then.

In March I record a soccer match between Wenchi and the neighbouring town of Tekiman, also the seat of a Head Chief. My diary reads, "Wenchi leading 3 goals to 1, so Tekiman removed the ball and the game ended." Shortly after this, our dog Salla, a lovely 'bush dog', died and though it had not bitten me, it was probable that it had licked my hand. Although there were no cuts on my hand, the fear of rabies was always in our mind. I had the dead animal sent in to Kumasi, where the medicos diagnosed rabies. I doubt if it was, but I think the doctors were scared of making a mistake and always erred on the safe side. Thus, at least officially, 'rabies' I might have, and so I went at once to Kumasi for a course of injections. On 5th May I had two injections in my tummy, and two a day thereafter till on the 25th I had the final pair. Some 40 injections in all, and they were given by an eccentric Scot. He complained, and probably rightly, about the equipment in the hospital. Nevertheless, it was not pleasant when, having tried ineffectively to jab the needle into my well-scarred tummy, he would withdraw it and remark, "Blunt again!"

So far I have not mentioned 'hammocks.' These were not the kind in use in the Navy, nor those for garden use in warm climates, but really more of a litter similar to those used in India for carrying notable personages around, and the same as those used in Ashanti for carrying Head Chiefs and Queen Mothers to Durbars. In early days some of the more rural stations had a complement of hammock carriers – 4 or 8, I forget which.

In Wenchi my predecessor regularly used a hammock rather than walk. I was still young and, apart from doses of malaria, very fit. I preferred walking. One day, however, I had gone on trek to a place in western Wenchi, travelling first by lorry, then by bicycle, and finally, when bicycling became impossible, on foot. But my temperature was 101° on arrival (with apologies that all these measurements are in Fahrenheit, the normal temperature in it being 98. 4°). I spent the next day in bed in the Rest House, then decided I must get back to Wenchi. The Rest House was not exactly a place of comfort. So I returned the next day and this time by hammock. I did not enjoy it, but at least the carriers carried me till I could reach a road and so proceed by lorry.

Still in July 1940. Believing I would be allowed to join up soon – hitherto DCs had been forbidden to do so – I then sold many of my personal possessions, and I gave my good double-barrelled gun to Kwasi as a sort of thank you for his splendid work over some 11 years. He really had been good. Never once did I lose anything. Nothing was ever stolen by any visitors or their servants, and not once did he give me food that made me ill. Considering the flies in the market and in the kitchen, this was truly remarkable.

On 10th July the Free French – 50 Europeans and 100 Africans – passed through Wenchi en route to Kumasi and beyond. The senior Madame was a real madam – as powerful as you can make them. I showed the group where they might camp, where the Rest House was, etc. I had six or seven to tea, several of them to drinks around 6 p.m., and then I invited Madame and half a dozen others to dinner. But, and this I found amusing, she insisted that I dine with them and be their guest. She insisted so I gave in, but then she asked if the dinner might be eaten in my house. "Of course," I said, "yes." Then she pointed out that my kitchen was better, so might the chicken be cooked in it, and by my cook? And so it went on. They came over for drinks and we had an excellent dinner in my house, but I am sure Madame felt she made an excellent hostess.

Then, alas, only a few days later I had yet another go of malaria. I drove to Kumasi on the 14th and went straight to hospital, where I remained for ten days. The Chief Commissioner then kindly had me to stay for a couple of days in the Residency ere I went to Accra and, at last, on 30th July, 1940, donned khaki, reported to cantonments, and the next day was a captain in the Gold Coast Regiment.

The two Battalions of the Gold Coast Regiment had already been increased to four – and the Brigadier asked me if I thought an Ashanti Battalion could be raised. This was a real 'teaser'. The Ashantis, throughout the last century, had been warlike, descending regularly on their southern neighbours and even warring with the British in 1874 and 1900. In the latter year they besieged the Governor in Kumasi. But their warfare was of a very African kind, accompanied by much noise of gunfire, drumming, shouting, and so on. Would the Ashanti make a good fighting soldier under strict discipline? There was the example of the Gold Coast Police to consider. As then constituted, it had two very distinct branches. The Blue branch was indeed recruited almost entirely from Ashanti and the Colony but this was the Clerical branch. The Khaki, or Escort Police, was a fine body of men who wore khaki blouses or jerseys, khaki shorts, puttees, and bare feet. (When playing hockey in Kumasi, any African who played would do so in bare feet.) These Escort Police, however, did not come from Ashanti but from the north, some from our own Northern Territories, and some, Mossis and others, from French colonies north of the Gold Coast. So could we raise an Ashanti Battalion in the Gold Coast Regiment?

I pondered this matter much, and discussed it with one or two other Ashanti DCs, and we thought it should be tried. This turned out to be an error of judgment. However, the Battalion was formed, I was posted to it, and we had to get on with it. Amongst the many recruits there were in fact very few Ashantis. Most were Northerners, including large numbers of Dagombas, but they merely joined to see what it was all about. They were not soldiers by tradition and, having joined and not liking it, they deserted – after every pay day. Now you might guess, if you do not know, that the Army pay sheet is no mere scrap of paper. Indeed, it is a huge sheet of paper that would cover any normal desk. And, of course, it had to be made up in triplicate. Ha, ha! Well, we had numerous 'desertions', in the Battalion, so to save trouble for others, they were all posted to my Company. Hence, while I had maybe 100 soldiers on parade, I had some 400 on my pay sheet. Of the 300 'deserters', probably 250 were Dagombas, and it seemed that all called themselves "Alasan Dagomba." I'm not sure if the penalty for desertion in wartime is death – it is probably so only under fire – but there was not a hope of catching them in any case. Not only did they have similar names, but also similar tribal markings, so that to a European they almost all looked alike.

My Company Clerk was one Kofi Genfi, an Ashanti from Kumasi. This is a tale about him. I saw him one afternoon working at these ghastly pay sheets and merely said, "These have to go in tomorrow." I looked down before Mess (we changed every night – not into mess kit but, because of mosquitoes, into long sleeves, trousers, and mosquito boots). I looked down again after dinner. "These go in tomorrow or you go out," I said. When I came down to parade next morning at 6 a.m., there he was, still at it, and a tiny hurricane lantern on the desk. But they were ready by 9 a.m. I had been hard on Kofi Genfi, but he thought I was fair and he liked me. Indeed, he used to write to me from Burma, where he went with the Battalion. "I was promoted Lance Corporal but I came home drunk, so was demoted." And again, "I was again promoted Lance-Corporal but hit the sergeant so was back to the ranks."

After Burma the Battalion stayed in India for a short while, but long enough for Kofi Genfi to become a member of a strange religion. When he returned to the Gold Coast, he used to wear a green hat – neither fez nor turban but vaguely Turkish. It was a religion no one had ever heard of. But we liked him and he was made a clerk in the Chief Commissioner's

Kofi Genfi's family

Office in Kumasi. Not for long, however, for we found he was in trouble with the police and had to dismiss him. He then made a small fortune running a sawmill business, but then he was too loyal an Ashanti. He annoyed Nkrumah and one evening Nkrumah's men came to arrest him. He was in his pyjamas but asked to go to the toilet where, as Kumasi then had no water-borne sewage system, there was the old fashioned bucket, withdrawn through a hole in the outside wall. Genfi hurriedly shoved the bucket out, followed it and, still in his pyjamas, ran and caught a taxi or at least a car that was for hire. He sped to the frontier and escaped to the French Ivory Coast, whence he wrote to me a long pathetic letter – still in his pyjamas and with no money. But he came back in due course, sent me Christmas cards from time to time, married (several wives), and had numerous children. And finally he wrote to me in 1994, with what few of us care to say – "I've made a success of my life." And, indeed, he then controlled a string of hotels. An amazing African – I am pleased to have known him.

Mention of Kofi Genfi's escape through the 'bucket hole' reminds me of three other incidents. Once, when the Governor and his family were visiting a station in Western Ashanti, I watched the lorry being unloaded and was amused to see that each member of the party had their own 'seat,' labelled 'Miss Alice,' 'Miss Jane' and so on. The second incident caused a furore in Accra. The wife of the Chief Justice wrote to the sanitary authorities: "Could not they come at another time as they always disturbed her when she was having her early morning cup of tea?" Back came the reply: "Cannot the lady concerned take her tea in another room?" The third incident had a similar effect. It was when the Colonial Secretary (or to be precise, it was actually his Deputy, the Under-Secretary) had, as was customary, minuted a communication to the Attorney-General, "For your opinion please." Back came the answer. This the Under-Secretary (unfortunately) minuted, "I cannot understand this." Back went the papers to the Attorney-General who wrote, "I can give the Under-Secretary reasons, but not understanding." I believe that Accra 'boiled' for weeks.

To revert to Kintampo, I may say that, following a good Naval custom not to drink spirits till sundown, the sun over the yard-arm, I only drank beer at midday, and never whisky till the evening. Well, one day the Ashanti Battalion – 7 G.C.R. – was visited by the G.O.C., General Giffard. While lunching in the Mess, he stressed that we should never drink whisky before lunch. Next morning, one of our Subalterns, admittedly rather a curious fellow, remarked, as he began breakfast with the usual brandy and soda, "Thank goodness he said nothing about drinking before breakfast."

And a last story from Kintampo. The Gold Coast Regiment at that time was officered entirely by Europeans. (The first Gold Coaster to be commissioned was in 1943). There were a number of those we knew as BNCOs – British Non-Commissioned Officers. While many of the officers were local like me, the BNCOs were often straight out from home and knew little of the African. One day I was watching a BNCO, who of course knew no native language, speaking through an interpreter. It was the usual sort of, "When I blow my whistle once, Section One goes forward, and Section Two gives covering fire. When I blow it twice, Section Two goes forward, and Section One gives covering fire." I asked the BNCO if he thought the interpreter understood what he had said. "Yes sir," he replied. So I asked the interpreter to repeat it to me. He gave the astonishing answer, "Master says, when we go to town, we wear jerseys, not blouses." Rather frightening, and it is really remarkable that these raw recruits, apart from Dagombas and others who would be deserting next pay day, were actually fit before too long to go to Burma, where they fought well.

Sadly I caught malaria again and this time the Medical Officer was of the opinion that, as I was having it so often, it was only a matter of time before I caught blackwater fever, which was almost always fatal. Indeed my cousin George Walker Russell, a Forest Officer in Northern Nigeria, did die of it. So it was decided to send me home. I regret to say that the medicos classified me as "not fit for employment even in a clerical or sedentary capacity," and said that it might be a long time ere I was fit again. I felt quite ashamed. But, again let's not forget . . . West Africa was, until not long ago, 'The White Man's Grave.' And so in the middle of November I motored to Kumasi, next day took the train to Accra, and went straight to hospital. I was there for a fortnight, and then on to Elder Dempster's *Abosso* for the journey home. Of the journey I would only mention that it was rougher than usual. The Bay of Biscay was really stormy, and in the saloon a large quantity of crockery as well as chairs, benches, and even windows, were smashed. Otherwise, no sign of U-boats. We landed in Liverpool, having gone there via the North of Ireland – the journey taking 18 days instead of the usual 12.

At Liverpool I caught the afternoon train at 2 p.m., but it was war time and the trains were not quite as punctual. It was 2 a.m. the next morning ere I arrived in Edinburgh – and was amazed to be met by both my parents as well as Elma and the child I had not yet seen. We reached my parents' house at 4 a.m., and our beds by 6. On leave, dear Aunt Madeline lent me a house opposite Alburne Knowe. This was 'Leven Bank,' where we made our home. My health steadily improved, but it was July 1941 before I felt really fit. Apparently both the Colonial Office and the Gold Coast Regiment had forgotten that I existed, so I wrote in and asked for a passage. Then, on 25th August, I was told to report in London next day. I was in London on the 26th, up to Liverpool next day, and by 2 p.m. on the 27th I was on Elder Dempster's *Abosso*. Quick work! I suppose I did not have anything to pack except a few clothes. Everything was secret and even my luggage had no address, only a number. I was not told where I was going, it was far too secret, but at Liverpool railway station the porter remarked – "You're for West Africa." He knew, but I was not supposed to know. I had been able to telephone my brother Victor, who was soldiering near Liverpool, that I expected to be there at 2 p.m., and in spite of all the secrecy, there were big notices up, "Captain Russell to report to . . ." There I found Victor, who, to my great joy, was able to tell my wife I was not off to China or America but back to West Africa.

It took two weeks to reach Freetown, Sierra Leone, instead of the usual nine days. Here we were transferred to a ghastly transport, HMT *Northumberland*. There were many of us, really crowded as was to be expected in war time. Down in the belly of the ship – hot, no breeze, stripped to the waist – I heard a neighbour remark, "so sticky, even the flies could not take off."

CHAPTER 8

Seventh Tour:
September 1941 – July 1943

Ten days later, 24 days in all instead of the usual 12, we arrived at Takoradi and then proceeded to Accra. This took three days. The Army had forgotten I existed, and so it remained. It was ten days ere I was given any work to do, and then merely a few route marches. But on 15th October 1941, I was given command of 'A' Company. (I presume this was still 7 Gold Coast Regiment, but regret that after 55 years I cannot remember). I paraded and had office work daily, even though living not in cantonments but in an Accra bungalow. Life was accompanied by the usual social activities, dinner parties, bathing, and so on. We also did much rifle range shooting and route marches of 15–18 miles starting at 4:30 a.m. These were all right in the cool of the morning, but not fun when the sun was up, for there was no shade on the Accra plains. We had our usual Caledonian dinner on St Andrew's Night, about 180 of us, which was worked off by the next four days under canvas.

Then the Governor, Sir Alan Burns, sent for me. He was soon to be not only Governor, Gold Coast, but also Acting Governor, Nigeria, charged with enforcing some co-ordination over all West Africa. One of West Africa's essential tasks was to accommodate large numbers of aircraft, some British but mainly American, flying from Belize in Brazil to Accra, then, via Kano in Nigeria up to Cairo. Nowadays we think of aircraft travelling non-stop distances such as China to UK but in 1941 the maximum distance was only 2–3,000 miles. British aircraft could, at great risk, fly from UK over Malta to Cairo, but for America the route was Belize-Accra-Cairo, plus many intermediate stopping places. Sir Alan Burns mentioned his responsibilities and said he wanted an ADC, etc., etc., and would I accept? He was not insistent but nearly so. I thought long and hard over it. I had always been a keen Territorial – must I now return to civilian duties? Eventually I agreed to his demands, rightly or wrongly. I often wish I had not, but there is no doubt that I had a job to do. For many months I had a hectic time, enjoyable but hard work, and indeed doing an essential task.

So, by the middle of December 1941 I had moved into Government House as Private Secretary and ADC Two days later, having gone to bed at 10 p.m., I was woken at midnight and spent the next two hours decoding a cable. And the following day, or rather only a few hours later, a garden party for 600 guests. This was followed by a small sherry party at the Castle. Then I went out to dinner followed by a cinema. Indeed it was hard work but, as when I had previously been at the Castle, a lot of fun as well.

One of the recreations I enjoyed was going out to the Accra Waterworks, the Reservoir and ancillary works at Weija. It was a large reservoir where we could boat, and there was a small pool for swimming and even a tennis court. But all this would be after a hard day's work, and not till the evening would we drive there. Near the Waterworks was a top secret small encampment. I said to the Governor as we returned one day, "Shall we go up and see what is there?" He thought he would not be allowed as it was so secret. But I thought I could manage. We got through the first sentry but the next one, a sergeant, beat me. When I asked if the Governor might drive up, he replied, "Governor? What of?" I suppose, coming from the UK, all he had heard of were Governors of Prisons. It just shows again what a lot of time it takes to get accustomed to another country.

In February, Sir Bernard Bourdillon, Governor of Nigeria, came to lunch, but really to hand over to Sir Alan Burns. At lunch I happened to remark: "I believe you play polo." To which he gave the gallant reply: "Yes, would you like my ponies while I am on leave?" And so it was that when we reached Lagos, I was able to use Sir Bernard's ponies, two for polo and a third for riding on non-polo days.

On 8th February 1942 we moved to Lagos. Sir Alan was sworn in and we settled in Government House. It was not a castle, as in the Gold Coast, but a large, suitable modern house and very comfortable. Here I was only to be Private Secretary, a Nigerian District Officer acting as ADC Lagos was on the air route to Cairo, and we had a continuous stream of Admirals, Generals, Royalty – British and foreign – stopping off and staying at Government House. Dinner parties were larger and grander than in Accra, but then Nigeria had a population of some 30 million against the Gold Coast's 5 million.

Once, if not twice, we had Sir Stafford Cripps to stay. He had been British Ambassador to Moscow and was a member of Churchill's war cabinet and Leader of the House of Commons. I still remember a dinner party on his first visit. There were some 30 or 40 of us, all in evening dress except for Sir Stafford, and a full three- or four-course dinner with accompanying wines was served. The dining room was gaily lit and Cripps commented on our circumstances, comparing them with the economies, black-outs and rationing back home, where people lived generally an austere life. He thought our behaviour extravagant. But frankly, why live in darkness, dress untidily, eat little, when the enemy was far away and we had no shortages? While we were entertaining Cripps and the 30 or so other guests, there was also a small dinner party upstairs for, I think, the King of Greece. There was also a third small party somewhere else for, perhaps, some of the King's bodyguard. All this in Lagos was on a much larger scale than I could have handled in Accra. Sir Stafford came to stay another time, coming, I think, from Moscow. He brought with him his daughter Peggy, who later married Joe Appiah in Kumasi. I will mention them again.

Work was fairly constant, mostly in the mornings and in the evenings. The afternoons were often free, and I was able to play polo twice a week on Sir Bernard Bourdillon's two ponies. Occasionally too I had a ride on the third pony he had lent me, but this was a wild beast that both bit and kicked the horse boy. I could not go near his head but he was not too bad once I had mounted, though at times he would buck and take me unaware. But one day we had General Anders, a senior Polish Commander, staying. I knew of his reputation as a horseman so I asked if he would like to see the ponies. I remember him walking up to this 'untouchable' beast and how the pony sensed a 'master.' He just quivered all over and let Anders play with him as he wished. It was a truly unique occasion. No one else ever managed to stroke him. The pony clearly knew Anders was Master of Horse.

The ADC was a Nigerian DO. In Nigeria those called District Commissioners in the Gold Coast were known as District Officers. He was a keen chess player. So, during the quiet parts of the day, usually between 2 and 4 p.m., we often played chess. When he retired, some 15 years later, he entered a firm which published chess books. He himself edited one book and gave me a copy which I treasure. Apart from chess, on the rare occasions we had a quiet evening, Sir Alan Burns enjoyed bridge and snooker. And, in the few free afternoons, we had tennis, golf, or bathing.

Again, life here, as in Accra, was busy. For example, after that large dinner for Cripps and Co., I was working late at night decoding a cypher telegram from the Secretary of State, and up at dawn or before to see off the Royal party at 5 a.m.. But, as I have indicated, there were many recompenses. Amongst other distinguished guests whom it was my privilege to meet, were a Director of the Bank of England, Prince Paul of Greece, Randolph Churchill, Viscount Samuel, Admiral Cunningham (the conqueror of the Mediterranean), Sir Harold Macmillan, the Duke of Gloucester, Eve Curie, Admiral Harwood and Sir Harold MacMichael.

Apart from governing – mainly a mass of office work – the Governor had time for two short trips. The first was up to Ibadan, the capital of the Yoruba of south-western Nigeria, who were involved in 1961 in that ghastly war with the Ibos of the southeast. Each army was commanded by a Sandhurst-trained officer. On our return, we passed through Abeokuta, one of the larger Yoruba towns. The other trip we had was quite different, really more of a relaxation: a boat trip through the inland waterways. We had a very comfortable 2-decker, Sir Alan and Lady Burns, the ADC, and myself, the usual household servants, and the ship's crew. We wandered for four or five days, seeing little except narrow channels often just big enough for us. Many had huge floating rafts of reeds called Sud; the upper parts of the White Nile are full of floating islands, which are known by the same name: the Sud of the Sudan. The ship was remarkably stable and when it was at anchor or tied up, we could even play bowls on deck.

On one occasion, when a general strike was threatened, His Excellency broadcast but only, I think, to Lagos. Then he came back to Government House and listened to it being repeated in Pidgin English, which we avoided in the Gold Coast but which was common in Lagos. When HE had said he was cross, the interpreter said: "That big man, he dey for Castle, he sick for belly too much" – at which we all, HE included, could only laugh.

After some five months of Lagos, Sir Bernard Bourdillon was soon to return. Personally, I was pleased to have seen another part of West Africa. At the end of June 1942, we all returned to Accra. There, to my great joy, I learned that Elma had managed to get a passage back. She arrived at Takoradi on 19th July. Things were not going to be simple. I, as ADC, had to be in almost continuous touch with Government House, and while I found this no problem, it was far from easy for Elma.

In Accra we now had rather more "VIPs" to be entertained. These included Lord Swinton, Secretary of State, the Maharajah of Indore, Lord Trenchard, Sir Zafrulla Khan and his Begum, and the Earl of Carlisle. And between these visits, HE went at least thrice on trek and, as I have written earlier, what a big exercise this usually was! I find I still have the programmes for these treks, printed well in advance and distributed to all concerned. My memory tells me that, after my long leave in 1941 I no longer suffered malaria, but my diary records illnesses on many occasions, days off, work, days in bed, and sometimes even the hospital. I might mention that in recent years I have tried to 'give blood,' but am always refused when it is learnt that I have had malaria, even though it is 40 years since my last attack. Elma and I did manage to escape to Winneba once for a sort of Local Leave. There we enjoyed doing little except some golf, tennis, swimming, and bird watching. But it was a happy ten days, more needed by Elma than by me.

On a trip to the Northern Territories with HE, we went out one day to the Veterinary Headquarters, run by an excellent Scot, Jock Stewart. He was a huge fellow and had played rugger for Edinburgh Academicals. He was a good friend of mine and he ran an excellent Cattle Station. There were many cattle, but he scarcely kept accounts. I had twice obtained cattle from him, two Ndama bulls to strengthen the cattle herd in Banda and a pair of cows to try them in a tsetse area. But he was thought to err financially so the auditors were sent up to enquire. The story goes that as the Director waved them good-bye he remarked: "They have spent five days here going through all my books, but never once counted a single head of cattle." Ever since then, I have treated auditors with scant respect. I could tell other tales of their failure to detect irregularities when alert District Commissioners spotted the flaws. And here is another story of Jock that you may not think funny, though I do. He was not a good driver, and one day had a small collision. The driver of the other car got out and expostulated for ages, getting louder and louder, Jock saying nothing. At last, when the other, a wee man, drew breath, Jock merely said: "Sorry, I didna ken you were just a beginner."

Prior to our ten-day trek to the North, I flew to Tamale and back in one day, for next day there was a garden party for 250 Girl Guides and I, as ADC, was responsible for all arrangements: police, car parking, teas, introductions, speeches, fours at tennis, and so on. And then the next day off for another ten days. It certainly was hectic, but I am sure I enjoyed it.

I have said that the Americans had a huge staging post for aircraft, flown from the USA to Brazil, to Accra, and so en route to Cairo. My diary records that one day I showed no less than six American Generals over the Castle, including of course the dungeons and the door whereby the slaves in bygone days were led out to the waiting ships. The next day HE entertained 200 British NCOs at a garden party. Indeed, life was not dull. My diary tells me that I read greatly, mainly Walter Scott or John Buchan. I must admit to having a partiality for Scots writers, and to being regretfully ignorant about the English classics.

And then, what a change again! Early in 1943 I was transferred back to District work and posted to Juaso, about 30 miles east of Kumasi. It was normal routine: much office but little court work, and the usual wandering around the District, mostly by car. But in April we had the full excitement of a riot in Kumawu. There had been disputes for a long time about the rightful succession to the 'Stool' (or throne – in Ashanti, *nkondwa*). The previous 'candidate' had been murdered; the Head Chief had already been charged with the crime and acquitted. The town was fairly equally divided, and being in forest or cocoa country, there was money and therefore many people owned guns.

While the police had the day-to-day responsibility for law and order, the District Commissioner had the overall responsibility for 'peace' in the area. I went out to ascertain the position. The village green was packed on all sides, fairly evenly divided between the two parties. There were about a dozen escort police keeping them apart. I walked out to the centre of the village green, smoked a pipe, and wondered what to do. While there, alone except for my orderly who always accompanied me, an old woman, bent and haggard, passed by me. She was muttering as she went in the vernacular – but I heard her say: "That's five of my sons he's killed now." One must remember that in Ashanti succession was matrilineal, and not patrilineal as in the UK. Chieftainship and other successions would normally pass not from father to son but from a man to his brother by the same mother (it is necessary to note this in a polygamous society), or to a sister's son. The Head Chief would normally come from the family of this old lady who had spoken to me. Clearly someone wanted one from a more distant kin group to succeed, and hence the murder, year after year, of her sons.

There were only a dozen or so police in Kumawu, so there was little positive action I could take. I asked the Chief Commissioner if he would let me have another score of police, but this was refused. I sadly left Kumawu, leaving the dozen police to try and keep some sort of peace. I returned there each of the following four or five days and luckily peace did prevail. A charge was preferred for murder but again there was an acquittal and I am sure that whoever did it would have enough friends to swear to an 'alibi.'

A few months later, staying at Kwamang, I heard of old rock carvings so I went to see them. Sure enough, in a cave I came across a number of interesting carvings, date unknown. As far as I know, these rock carvings I had 'discovered' – I think this is the right word – were the only ones in the Gold Coast, but they were not really ancient, maybe only a few hundred years old.

Again I had a short spell in Kumasi Hospital. There I met two doctors working with the Royal Army Medical Corps, both out from Britain. They told me they had shot one of those pretty white egrets, technically buff-backed herons, and, on examination, had found it quite fit but to be a carrier of "Malaria, Philaria, Hookworm, Flukes, and suspected Yellow Fever." To carry all this – and remain fit! No wonder human beings were subject to sickness in West Africa. Think of a mosquito biting an egret, then biting a human being. Luckily, this did not often happen.

On emerging from Kumasi hospital, I was sent to hospital in Accra, then spent a night at Government House and so on to Sekondi to await a ship to take me home on leave after a long tour of 21 months. But this was still wartime and I was fortunate in being sent to the UK and not, like so many others, to South Africa. Boats, however, were scarce. Elder Dempster had already lost several. After a week of idleness, I was put on board the *Adrastes*, a vessel of 8,000 tons with a Chinese crew but no doctor aboard. I suppose this did not matter, as we would be sailing in convoy and a doctor, if required, could be brought from another boat. The next day we sailed, 15 ships in the convoy and travelling at the "rate of the slowest ship," which was 7 knots. This is really slow. It took us a week to reach Sierra Leone where, in Freetown's large harbour, ships would wait to be grouped into suitable convoys. After four days off Freetown we left, now 35 ships, but still at only 8 knots. Ten days later our escort had risen to 15 ships, mostly small boats, and the next day a cruiser was added. It was just in time. The Admiralty knew what it was about, for the next day we were spotted by a

German Focke-Wolfe. It only dropped bombs once and we were delighted to see a Hurricane catapulted off to give chase.

One day Elma and I watched, with our binoculars, a Liberator chase and sink a German plane. It was fascinating to watch the cruiser, obviously the main target from the enemy's point of view. We saw the German plane release a bomb from a great height and then the cruiser swiftly take evasive action – successful every time. Later, another cruiser was added to our escort and enemy planes were common, but not one of our ships was lost. A month after leaving Takoradi (2nd July to 2nd August) we found ourselves in, of all places, Loch Ewe by Ullapool, and two days later, to our great joy and delight, docked in Methil, Fife. It was perfect for us and we went straight to Edinburgh.

Leave was spent with our parents till the end of the year, when we again took a lease of Leven Bank. Then, early in 1944, I returned to the Gold Coast. Leaving Elma at Leven Bank on 12th January, I took the train to Edinburgh, and later the 10 p.m. night train to Liverpool, with, as another passenger, my cousin, Arthur Russell. We took the usual breakfast at the Adelphi and sailed in the afternoon of the 13th.

My diary records nothing of the voyage. Perhaps we were told not to make records in case we were torpedoed and our notes might give away information, for example, numbers of ships in convoy, speed, escorts, etc. Anyhow, my diary is a complete blank except for, quite uselessly, recording bridge and chess wins and losses.

CHAPTER 9

Eighth Tour:
February 1944 – May 1945

So, a full month after leaving Scotland, I disembarked at Takoradi, went by train to Kumasi, and had a full tour of 15 months in Wenchi ahead of me. How happy I was to be back in my beloved Wenchi, with Arthur Russell in Sunyani, only fifty miles away and easy to meet for weekends, etc. But, alas, Elma was not with me for the whole tour. Otherwise it was very enjoyable.

One task that took much time was the maintenance of roads. I had 150 miles to maintain, all gravel roads but in good order, and my workforce was one man per mile. I also had one overseer, one truck, and a budget based on paying the labourers 1s. a day for a 26-day month, that is, 26s. per man per month. I tried to encourage the 150 men to save. Indeed, nearly 100 of them did so and of the 26s. I paid them, they would pay back 5s. for me to put into their Post Office Savings Books. The scheme worked well. I also tried to inspect the men at work in the middle of the month and then pay them towards the end. This meant carrying much money around. At times I had £800 in florins: quite a weight! After, maybe, six months or so, I came to know nearly half the 150 labourers by name and sight.

I will relate the story of Yaw Mo, one of the roadmen. 'Yaw' meant born on a Thursday, and 'Mo' was the area he came from. He had always been a friend of mine but was not always well. So when he absented himself, I was worried. I sought him out and asked the other labourers, but no word of him. Then, one day, perhaps six to eight months later, driving along a 'bush' road (that is, not one that I maintained but a Chief's road and only just motorable), I spotted him. I stopped the car, my small Ford lorry, and called to him. He ran to me then said: "Wait till I get my fire." You remember the Old Testament story of Abraham about to sacrifice Isaac and Isaac saying: "I see the wood and fire, where is the sacrifice?" Well, here was Yaw Mo: "Wait till I get my fire." Back he ran and brought a smouldering log. I offered him money and told him I had some 25 shillings due to him. He replied, "No, thank you," and held out a wee potato. "I have food for today," he said. He undid a corner of cloth, the sort of toga all the Africans wore, and added, "Here I have another potato for tomorrow and then I shall be home" – 30 miles away. The smouldering log meant he was able to cook the potatoes whenever he wished, and was not dependent upon anyone else. This story of Yaw Mo certainly helped to make clear Isaac's remark, "I see the fire."

During this tour I often rode horses from the Zongo. The owners seldom did so and I think they were pleased to see me ride and, no doubt, to receive a little money in thanks. One weekend Arthur Russell and his wife Jean, at whose wedding I had assisted not long before, came to stay. We went out for a ride but as we were cantering slowly along the road, a pig came out and brought Jean's horse crashing. When Arthur and I reached her she was unconscious and also a queer sight. It was a hot evening. We were perspiring, and so the dust from the road clang easily to Jean and we could scarcely make out her face. I galloped back to my bungalow and brought my car and a couple of boys. When we arrived, Jean was at least conscious. We drove her at once to my house, but her arm was obviously broken or dislocated. There were no other Europeans in Wenchi, so we sent for the local bone setter. He came but was too frightened to play with a white person's bones, so we could do nil except drug Jean and contact an Army doctor at Kintampo, 50 miles away. He came early next morning and set the bones back in place. No harm done, but I often think of the pain on Jean's face as the African tried 'gently' to set the elbow, and of the bone setter's face, afraid to be rough with a white person.

One of my guests who stayed with me several times was a Mrs M. She was doing an historical study of the different tribes or clans in Western Ashanti. They were all within the Ashanti Confederacy. If there was a Durbar called by Nana Prempeh, the Asantehene or King of Ashanti, they must attend. Some of these tribes, however, especially Doma and Tekiman, had fought against the Ashantis in the latter half of the last century and Mrs M. endeavoured to prove they were not Ashantis and should not be in the Ashanti Confederacy. I naturally hoped to see them remain within the Confederacy, increasing the stature or status of the Ashantis. Kwame Nkrumah and others backed Doma and Tekiman, letting them form a strange 'Brong' alliance. I regretted having had Mrs M. to stay.

We had a Court of Assize in Wenchi one day. The judge from Kumasi came to try a murder case there, to save the witnesses from having to travel to Kumasi. It was a formal occasion and for the opening of the Assize I put on my white uniform, sword, etc. I think this was a good idea, showing what the British thought of justice, and I guess that the rulers of Ghana today will be behaving in much the same way.

One day I motored to Banda, the tribe I liked so much. Hitherto I had always arrived on foot, but a road – just motorable and no more – had been opened a few days before. I went, as usual, to greet the Head Chief. He just shook hands and said, "I will take you to the Rest House and we will talk tomorrow." When I said I was not staying, he could not understand. I had always stayed at least one night, usually three or four. What had gone wrong? He was disturbed. Then when I remarked that I was going on to Berekum, some 70 miles away "to sleep," they all laughed. "The DC is in a funny humour today." To them, it was a four days' walk, and I was going to do it before nightfall. Ha! Ha! I remember well their faces, their looks of astonishment and disbelief.

I also remember one small meeting we had with a Chief when I was accompanying the Governor on a tour of Western Ashanti. The Governor and I sat on chairs under vast umbrellas that the Chief had provided. The Chief had, as was customary, given the Governor as a present a cow – or bullock. (On informal occasions a DC would be given a chicken and eggs, on formal occasions a sheep, and to the Governor it would be a cow). The Governor was giving his usual short chatty speech, and it was, as usual, interpreted – and each time the Governor paused to let the interpreter have his say, the cow gave a loud moan – indeed, it happened so often that it appeared to the Governor that the cow knew what was in store.

Here is another story of my work as District Commissioner, Wenchi. As I entered my office one morning, I noticed a few wild Northerners sitting on the verandah. Soon after, my clerk came in. He was accompanied by the Sanitary Inspector, who had a note in his hand. It was asking my authority for the burial of a bullock and he asked me to sign it. "Sir," he said, "it was sick and cannot be sold in the market." Just then the North-erners entered. There was nothing wrong with the beast, they claimed. What was I to do? Usually I took the Sanitary Inspector's word, but this time it was being queried, and the nearest doctor was 100 miles away. If I said, "Sell the bullock," and then people ate it and died, wouldn't I look guilty? It was then that I noticed Kwasi returning to my bungalow from the market, having gone there – as he did every day – to buy a bone to make soup for my lunch. Incidentally, the soup never varied from day to day. I would ask Kwasi "What kind of soup do we have today?" His answer was always the same: "We have just soup." But to return to the story. I called Kwasi and asked him if he thought the bullock meat was bad. He studied it carefully and replied that it was perfectly good. Now over fifteen years or so Kwasi had never given me bad meat, so I thought he knew what he was talking about. I took a gamble and allowed the meat to be sold in the market, but thinking what a risk I had taken. Later Kwasi told me the full story. A Northerner had 'misbehaved' with a friend of the Sanitary Inspector. "You wait till the next time you kill a bullock," the Inspector is reported to have said. Kwasi also told me that he had never been able to give me a certain bit of meat as the Inspector always took it for himself. There was no doubt that Wenchi presented me with problems that could not be solved by anything I had learned at Harrow or at Oxford, or indeed on our short Tropical Services Course!

One of my duties, during the War, was to pay allowances to soldiers' wives, some 15s. monthly. This did not happen often as few natives of Wenchi had enlisted. But one afternoon or evening I was in Sampa, sitting as usual with the Chief and his Elders, and with most of the villagers, say 150 of them, in the room. A soldier on leave happened to be there so I called out both him and his "wife." There seemed to be a strange quiet in the hall so I thought I would have some fun. "Is this your wife?" I asked. "How long have you been married?" "Do you have any children?" At each question and answer there was a stir in the room but no one spoke, so I said I would see the two the next morning. That evening I learnt that the woman was not his wife but his sister. The evening's farce had nothing to do with black versus white, nor do I even think it was a matter of, "What can we get from the Government?" Rather, I think they were testing me, their District Commissioner. Had I paid the 15s., my reputation would have been seriously undermined.

There was another trick we had to contend with. This was the African's – like the Oriental's – wish always to give an answer that pleases. One morning I attended a large meeting in Wenchi. It was their Annual Estimates session.

Sitting by the Head Chief, I remarked, "Why is not your Inspector of Police here?" The reply came quick as a flash: "I sent him on a message." Even as the Chief spoke, the Inspector stepped into the room, having been outside smoking a cigarette. Then I asked, "Where is the sergeant?" The reply, "He is sick," but again as he spoke the 'sick' man entered the hall. Basically, it is a sign of weakness ever to admit, "I don't know." Here is another case. I remarked to my clerk one day, "When the Chief of X asked me to say that he was honest, do you think his standard of honesty is the same as mine?" My clerk replied, "No sir, our standard is a bit limited."

My diary records every day as being full. Although on the outer fringe of Ashanti, we had masses of visitors and indeed, life was full – as it should be. And most enjoyable! One of my not infrequent guests was the magistrate from Kumasi. He visited me probably monthly. And there was an African, WB Van Lare, who also served as magistrate in Kumasi and was a friend of many of us. He later became a judge of the Supreme Court, and ended his career as Ghana's High Commissioner to Canada.

Now for a different sort of story. All DCs were encouraged to study the history of the tribes among whom they worked. A belief of all Ashantis was that originally they "came down a ladder from heaven" or "came out of a hole in the ground." Land ownership was vital to all Ashantis and the universal belief was that whoever arrived first was the owner. Thus the point of the origin myths (if I may call them that) about descending by the ladder or emerging from the hole was that the new arrivals found no one in the area and so it became inalienably theirs. It is maybe difficult to understand in over-crowded Britain, where we have title deeds to all land, that in parts of Africa, and indeed parts of Wenchi, there was much empty land. So the first 'settlers' could rightly claim it, there being no opposition. Such 'holes' referred to in the fables were very sacred and known only to few. The Wenchi 'hole' I longed to see. Having been stationed in Wenchi several times, the Wenchihene and his Elders knew and trusted me. Nevertheless it took many evenings of asking the Wenchihene ere he finally consented to show me the place. It was a big occasion when the Elders at last agreed. We set off one day to try and find it. Incidentally, as we walked along, we crossed a tiny track and the Wenchihene, taking my arm, remarked in Twi, for he spoke no English, "As a boy I ran madly along this track, the Ashantis chasing me," – and that would have been only some 45 years previously.

There was no path to the 'hole' for us to take. It was really 'history', and hardly anyone in the whole tribe had ever been to the spot. Maybe some fifty of us wandered for ages through the dense forest, almost jungle, till someone said, "This is it," and there in front of us lay a clear circle of bare earth. Yes, this was the spot! We all had a drink of palm wine – quite pleasant if nearly fresh, but not so nice and very strong when a few days old. Some time later I persuaded the Elders to pay the spot a second visit, this time with some labourers and picks and shovels. This was very successful. After much digging and several hours work, earth had been removed to a depth of some 12–15 feet and at the bottom there were indeed signs of a 'hole' or tunnel. In the course of a third visit, digging at the bottom, the labourers actually found a tunnel and I even entered it! The fourth and last time I went there, accompanied by my cousin Arthur Russell, I walked several yards into the tunnel. There was, however, no air. Matches would not light. Indeed, I felt ill after each entry, but I had seen signs of the tunnel extending several yards further on. This is the end of the story, for no-one has been able to explain to me how there could be a tunnel there. Was it an old water-course? It was a problem but at least it did prove that the Wenchis really did have a 'hole' to fit in with their story of their early origins.

Having succeeded in persuading the Wenchis to let me see their 'hole,' I next tackled a nearby tribe – let's call it N. Eventually they too agreed and, accompanied by the usual Elders and a sheep or two for the customary sacrificial slaughter, led me to their 'hole.' The 'hole' itself was disappointing, but again there was a 'hole' and I and the Elders were satisfied that this fitted in with their tribal history. On the way back, walking with two youths, they said to me:- "You are only the third stranger to have seen the 'hole' – and the other two are dead." I thanked them, and said that they might have told me this before I visited the place. But they assured me that as I was white, I would not be killed. However, a strange thing happened not long after. The Chief became ill and after a while was taken into hospital in Kumasi. He lay there dying. A Scots lady doctor told me that the Chief was mortally ill but that he suffered from no known disease. In fact she and I agreed that "fetish had been put on him," and in consequence he would assuredly die. I still feel that I may have been the cause of his death, in that he had taken someone other than a member of his tribe to see their most sacred spot.

I have mentioned my boys Kwasi and Kofi. The latter was 'bright' and soon took over my car. At first he just cleaned it, then checked oil, water, etc., then drove it to the front door . . . and so on till, all on his own, he had learnt well. He really was not only a bright but a likeable kid, and I would take him with me on the front passenger seat on long journeys. When traffic was negligible and we met another vehicle only every few miles, I would read a book or papers while he would steer till he saw an oncoming vehicle. Then he would say, "Master, car come," and I would take over. This is maybe not to be recommended, certainly not in Britain, but where traffic was so rare it enabled me to do much preparation before meetings.

It was during this tour that I first met Nana Kofi Busia or Dr Busia. He was a native of Wenchi, later to become leader of the Ashanti National Liberation Movement and so Leader of the Opposition. Then, after one of the many coups West Africa was always having, he became Prime Minister of Ghana. Being a Wenchi, and knowing my love for Wenchi, he and I became firm friends from this period.

Elma had stayed at home to tend our two children but by April 1945 Barbara, the elder, was seriously ill. On 8th May – VE Day – I received a cable that her condition was grave. I decided to fly home. I packed the next day, travelled to Kumasi on the 10th, by train to Sekondi on the 11th, and the next day was 'weighed' – in the early days of flying, passengers, as well as their luggage, had to be carefully weighed. On the 13th we flew to Freetown where my sister was, and then on to Bathurst for the night. On the 14th we stopped at St Etienne and Rabat, and stayed the night in Lisbon. On the 15th another flight of six hours brought us to Hurn airport. It had taken three days by air from the Gold Coast to London. Sadly, the wee girl died of leukaemia in August. I had the leave I was due and then in December flew back the same slow route: from London I took the train to Bournemouth where I spent the night, then up very early next morning to fly via Lisbon to Rabat for the night, then via St Etienne to Bathurst for the night, then to Sierra Leone for the night, arriving at Takoradi the evening of the next day. So this was four days of flying and five days in all since leaving London.

Ninth Tour:
December 1945 – June 1947

Happily back in Wenchi late in December 1945, I had my sister from Sierra Leone to spend Christmas with me. We also entertained a friend of mine, a very able member of the British Council but also rather naughty. There was a health scare. I forget what it was, but traffic between Ashanti and the Northern Territories was forbidden. However, this bright lady managed to persuade the Chief Commissioner of Ashanti that the Chief Commissioner of the Northern Territories had agreed to her passage – and had equally persuaded the latter that the former had agreed to her going north. As I said, rather naughty! She was hoping to travel to the Niger, then west along the river to its source, and so end up in Bathurst, the westerly point of Africa. All she had was a steward boy – in those days we never travelled without a servant or servants – and a tooth brush. She did not even have a camp bath. We lent – or I should say gave – her one which had belonged to my father in World War I. We also found her lots of food and wondered how far she would get. Marvellously, she made it all the way. She was later to become Lady Monson, and if you knew her you will not be surprised that she succeeded.

I should make a brief mention of my efforts for Edinburgh Zoo. One day at Christiansborg Castle I noticed some of those brightly coloured touracos which Sir Alan Burns was tending; "Why?" I asked. His reply was that he was hoping to collect a number of attractive birds, keep them for a while in the Castle, and then send them to London Zoo. As Sir Alan Burns had a good Scots name, and indeed his grandfather came from St Andrews, and as he was collecting for London, I thought the least I could do was collect for Edinburgh. I spoke to Mr Gillespie, then Director-Secretary of Edinburgh Zoo. Mr Gillespie was delighted – yes, they would be glad of anything I could collect, particularly since by the end of the War, the Zoo had been denuded of almost all its livestock. I have written several accounts of 'Collecting for a Zoo' both in Edinburgh zoological magazines and the *Nigerian Field* but briefly, over a dozen years or so in all, I sent numerous animals and birds to Edinburgh Zoo (see Appendix V). I kept many aviaries of very different sizes. I often had three full-time 'keepers' – and I collected throughout any District I was in. The collecting was done by my roadmen (sometimes I had as many as 150) and also by the Chiefs – indeed, by anyone. I paid for the aviaries and for the keepers, and my expenses were refunded by the Zoo. I made nothing out of all the work – and it took a lot of time. I was able to have free transport by road and rail in the Gold Coast. Thereafter the Zoo was responsible for transport to the UK and up to Edinburgh. One of our Forest Officers was George Cansdale, who also collected for London (and indeed became Manager/Director of London Zoo on his retiral). We used often to swap species from our collections. I expect to write more later on about the Zoo – but this is to let you know how it all began.

I wrote earlier about how I would drive and read a book while Kofi steered. Often when travelling with Sir Alan Burns, either as his ADC or as a DC, he and I would sit in the back of the car and play chess on my portable chess board. When we came near a village, or there were people lining the road, the Orderly would warn us and HE would don his hat and salute graciously to the waiting crowds.

In February 1946, Elma and Margaret (aged 2) arrived. One day we visited Kintampo and naturally went to greet my great friend, Sarikin Fanyinamah Wangara, the ex-slave trader but now benign chief. He had met Elma before but he had never seen a white child. When I took her to the Sarikin, he lifted her up on high at arm's length to have a real thorough inspection of this strange object, a white babe. Quite alarming, but to my intense pride Margaret never whimpered, though she might well have done so.

I mentioned earlier that Elma and I surveyed the road to Bedu, saving them several miles. One day on this tour the Bedu people had the official opening of the new realigned road and after it they gave a golden pendant and bracelet to Elma and to me a gold tiepin, Ashanti stool, leopard skin and the usual turkey, three large baskets of fruit, and 200 eggs (probably all were ancient and inedible – but none the less a kindly gesture).

On 18th May my diary records, "Owusu-Sarpong's funeral." I mention this because 50 years later his son, now head of a faculty at the University of Science and Technology in Kumasi, wrote to me and reminded me how kind I had been that day.

We were privileged to have Sir Alan and Lady Burns to stay. Usually all senior Europeans and Africans would be invited to dine, but as we were alone in Wenchi we had a delightfully quiet evening. They, of course, as was the custom, stayed in my house and Elma, Margaret and I moved to the Rest House.

One day Elma and I (and, of course, Margaret) rose early and motored to Kumasi and on to Accra (say, 300 miles). A punishing day, but we were soon refreshed as we stayed in the Castle. I should say how kind Sir Alan and Lady Burns always were. Then, two days later, we rose again at about 4 a.m. and motored back to Kumasi and on to Wenchi. My diary records, "a tough life for Elma," and indeed it was, especially as I was so often on trek in the district. She (and Margaret) would have the help of perhaps two boys, a gardener, and so on, and it was quite safe: there was no fear of anyone thinking of being a 'nuisance.'

On 8th June, when 'VE Day' was officially celebrated, I attended Durbars at the three towns of the Head Chiefs – Wenchi, Tekiman and then Nkoranza: indeed, a full day. My diary records, "Wenchihene comes to my bungalow and gives me a pin and ring and a necklace for Margaret (all of course in gold)." I mention this just as an example of the continual kindness of the Ashanti.

In June I was transferred to Kumasi as District Commissioner there. I was sad to leave Wenchi, but I was becoming more senior and had to be tested in a bigger District. It was very different to life in Wenchi. In Kumasi we were social, very social (as was everyone in the town). There were parties for drinks (6.30 to 8), and dinners at home or out almost every night. Tiring – but good fun. Among the guests, the Asantehene came to dine occasionally.

One day I recorded rising at 2.30 a.m., leaving Kumasi at 3, reaching Kintampo by 7, making a formal presentation of the King's Medal for African Chiefs to my friend the Sarikin Fanyinamah, then having breakfast in the Kintampo Officers Mess, meeting the Chief Commissioner, Ashanti, arriving back in Kumasi by 5 p.m., dining with Elma, then going to a cinema, having someone in for drinks, and then someone else to stay. It was certainly a full life! And two days later I saw off 20 crates (which I had had specially made) of birds and animals for Edinburgh Zoo. Another

Kumasi Durbar, 1946

day I recorded playing five games of squash (Regimental squash court), then having dinner with guests including the CCA and the Brigadier.

One of my responsibilities had to do with the Kumasi Town Council. As District Commissioner I was automatically President. It took up a lot of time but, as is so often the case when everything is going well, nothing seems to matter. The problem is when things go wrong. And one day they did. His Excellency was touring Ashanti, and there was one day in Kumasi when the CCA was with him and so was I, as District Commissioner. As we were wandering about on foot, HE suddenly said to me: "Russell, that building is on fire – see how long it will take to put it out." I despatched a clerk to call the fire engine as quickly as possible. It came and found a hydrant, affixed a length of hose, and ran out the other end to the building 'on fire.' So far I was rather pleased. But, alas, no water came. After about three minutes a tiny trickle appeared at the end of the hose, about enough

Kumasi Durbar, 1946. Asantehene and the Golden Stool

to wash one's teeth. I felt deeply ashamed, and the Governor was rightly cross with me – but I had learnt a lesson.

Towards the end of 1946 I started the Kumasi Dining Club, modelled on one they had in Accra. We had 18 members – 9 black, 9 white. The white members included heads of departments and heads of trading firms, and the black members, the Asantehene, three other Head Chiefs, three or four lawyers (including a judge), maybe two doctors, and one or two senior politicians. It was a great success. We dined once every two months, and it was a marvellous way of getting to know and trust each other.

On 12th December there was to be a Durbar – a big one, with all the Head Chiefs in Ashanti present (I have a video of it). I, as DC, was responsible for many of the arrangements. Even the Chief Commissioner came down twice to see how things were to be, and the Governor on arrival in Kumasi also had a thorough inspection – to see where he was to stand, how to greet the Chiefs, how they would return his greetings, etc., etc. (My only regret was that Elma was unable to be present – but she watched it all from the hospital where Catherine was to be born three days later). I was present at the Durbar (in uniform) from 8 a.m. till 1 p.m. and even the Governor was there for four hours. I estimated that there were 150 large umbrellas. And not only the Asantehene and the Queen Mother were there, but, most rare, most precious, most revered – the Golden Stool was on display. In the evening I was among the 150 guests His Excellency entertained to drinks at the Residency, and then I entertained the Ashanti DCs (who included two Africans) and their wives to dinner, a party of 16 of us. Again, I can only say, a full life, with plenty of hard work and plenty of relaxation to follow.

At that time I must have been acting District Commissioner, Kumasi, for when the substantive DC returned from leave I was posted to Bekwai, a delightful district some 20 miles south of Kumasi, where I occupied a brand new bungalow, entirely mosquito-proofed (thus no need for long sleeves and mosquito boots in the evening) and having two huge rainwater tanks (and so never a shortage). My 'staff' was now Dubbie, Kofi, a cook, a nanny (Jemima), a laundry man (on 30s. a month), two gardeners, and three keepers for my livestock (destined for Edinburgh Zoo).

I had moved to Bekwai in late December 1946 and my 1947 diary is, thankfully, now in biro and much more legible. I suppose biros had only then reached us. Work at Bekwai was similar to that in other Districts but being in the forest country, with cocoa everywhere, the local people were healthy and wealthy (in comparison with the North or even the Coastal belt). I trekked frequently, but usually just for day trips, the area being so much smaller than North-West Ashanti and the roads ever so much better. In fact I had hardly any roads to maintain, and with the magistrate taking all the court work, my work was now almost entirely with the 'Local Authority,' that is, the Chiefs and Elders. I had to encourage them to bring 'young men' – meaning non-chiefs – on to their councils, to raise taxes (none at all existed), and to supervise their native courts. So much of what follows will tell of amusing and interesting events – but little of my work.

I remember one evening staying at Denyase and being invited to their village dance in the evening. It was held on the rather uneven football pitch but the Chief and his Elders sat on a pleasant dais where I joined them. After the Chief returned from a dance, I enquired if he had been dancing with one of his wives. "Oh no," he replied, and pointed to behind his chair where the wives stood to supervise his conduct. He had recently come to the Stool, so I asked if he had inherited many stool wives. He replied, "Yes, but I sacked the lot. I took on fresh ones – four in use and three in training." (My mother always thought this my best Gold Coast story).

Another of my visits was to the same town, Denyase. This time it was in the morning and the Chief and Elders sat in the usual half-circle. The custom was that I walked round greeting each Chief or Elder in person with a handshake. While doing so I noticed that each and all were glancing down at my trousers. I was wearing white shorts and white hose – rather smart, and I knew that they were clean that morning. So what was it? I carefully looked down and saw a wee thing wagging out of the trouser pocket. The cause? As you know, I kept many animals for Edinburgh Zoo and amongst them several varieties of squirrel. My house being totally mosquito-proofed, there was no need to build so many aviaries, and a small Green Squirrel lived in and around my dining room. That morning at breakfast it had been over inquisitive, and was eating rather much of my bacon-and-eggs, so I just put it in my trouser pocket, where it fell asleep – but woke up a few hours later as I circled the Denyase chiefs and let its tail wag! It caused a lot of amusement.

One of the DC's duties was not only wandering around his District during the day, but attending 'social' functions in the evening. Once, at a village near Lake Bosumtwi, I was attending an evening dance: the dances were both native and English. I did not dance but, sitting usually next to the Chief, I met many people. This evening there was a very smart and beautifully dressed man with white hair dancing. Surely, I thought, I must know him, but no, I could not place him. I asked the Chief who he was. "Sir," he said, and burst out laughing, "that is your cook." Someone else added, "and he is probably wearing your dinner jacket."

Only a few miles from Bekwai was a small virgin forest, virgin because it was sacred (probably an old burial ground). While there was still much forest in Ashanti, there was little original forest outside our excellent Forest Reserves. But here, near Bekwai, there was a quite untouched forest, and hereto came many monkeys – not only the common ones (diana, mona, puttynose, of which I sent many to Edinburgh), but also the large handsome white-tailed colobus, becoming rarer as its skin was a valuable commercial export, and in addition, the much rarer Red Colobus. It was my regular pleasure to take any guests I had staying with me out to see these handsome primates. Sometimes we saw none, but one day I recorded seeing, in a short space of half an hour, 20 white and 12 red colobus, as well as several mona monkeys. A real treat!

I must mention being visited by three Members of Parliament. I met them and took them to Obuasi, to the rich Ashanti Goldfields Corporation where, among other sights, we watched labourers (strong men from the North) pushing wheelbarrow loads of soil to help level a football field. They then placed the empty wheelbarrows on their heads, walking back for another load. The MPs thought this well worth seeing. They came back to tea, and I still remember them on the floor playing tiddlywinks with my daughter, aged three. Next morning I took the MPs to Fomena to see how a Native Court administered justice. I took them in to the court and the four of us sat down. Then the proceedings commenced. The Court Crier made his wild and continuous cries, all in the vernacular: "Listen to the Chief. Hear. Hear. Listen all ye who hear . . ." It was non-stop, in a loud yet almost squeaky voice, the Crier – small like a dwarf – sitting on the floor. To me this was 'normal,' that is, customary, but to the visitors it was more than they could take. Mr Errol (soon to be Principal of a Cambridge College) and Mr Callaghan (later to be Prime Minister) had their handkerchiefs in their mouths and had their heads down between their knees. It was funnier than they could take. I am reminded too of the time I took them round the maternity wing of the Obuasi hospital, and the quick retorts of these MPs. One (I won't say which) remarked, "What a beautiful baby," and the other replied, "A typical stupid remark – can't you see it's premature, only weighs three pounds?"

One day I was, as was customary, visiting a Chief and Elders and, having greeted them, I sat amongst them and, while discussing 'politics,' idly glanced through their court record books, the Treasury Account Books and so forth. Noticing one case where they had fined a person only 10s. for mosquito larvae, I asked the Chief, "Why only 10s.? The usual fine is £1, "To this he replied, "We did fine him £1." While this was going on, I noticed a person at the far side of the meeting slinking away. I thought it might be the Court Clerk so I made my apologies, nipped into my car, and raced to the court house, just beating the Court Clerk – for it was he – who was on his bicycle. The point of this story is that while the Chief and Elders were all illiterate, only the Court Clerk was literate. The accused had been fined £1, but the record book read 10s., as did the cash book, as did the ledger, and even the receipt book – cardboard having been inserted between the original receipt for £1, given to the accused, and the carbon copy which read 10s. The Clerk had pocketed the other 10s. And indeed, it was audit proof: everything tallied. The Clerk could have gone on defrauding the public had not I asked the Chief and Elders about the case. Naturally I reported the offender to the police, but asked them not to prosecute. The criminal was about the only literate in the area and I did not think he would dare defraud again.

Here is another story of how the DC must be alert. I was once accompanying the Governor around Cape Coast. He was looking over the store of an interesting 'local' who was asking for a small grant to purchase machinery for his work. "Do you get much work?" asked the Governor. "Oh, yes," the man replied, and showed His Excellency his 'order book,' ready and open at the day's date and a mass of entries – all very impressive. When they had gone on to the next room, I nipped back and had a closer look at the book. Yes, the day's date was full of 'orders,' but there was not another entry in the whole book. Every other page was blank. It was all totally bogus, as I had suspected. But I took no action. Fraudulent as the book may have been, the man was actually doing a good job. And this reminds me of another delightful 'rascal,' this time from Accra. He ordered large quantities of material from Japan and at the head of his notepaper was a picture of Christiansborg Castle, the Governor's residence – but giving the impression that this was his house! But the Japanese suppliers were equally dishonest. Their reply was intercepted: "How do you wish the articles to be marked. Japanese? British? Foreign?"

A bird I had tried to collect unsuccessfully was at last being offered to me (at the high price of £1). This was a golden oriole, a most beautiful golden yellow bird with a melodious voice. I thought they were purely fruit eaters, but one day I saw one actually eating one of the small finches I had put in the same aviary. After that all the orioles were kept by themselves. One day, to my real sorrow, all five in one aviary escaped. I expect the keeper had been careless when entering to feed them. I watched where they went – one to a tree not far off. As it was nearly sunset, we hoped he would sleep soundly there. Soon after sunset we carried over a ladder, saw the oriole asleep with its head tucked under its wing, and one of my keepers was able to catch it. The next day another of the escapees was seen circling round. We opened the aviary door and sure enough it entered. It was hungry. I am not trying to defend zoos in principle, but to give this example of an animal being reasonably happy if it is sure of food and shelter.

In March 1947 Elma with our two daughters sailed for home and three months later I too sailed – but not alone. I was accompanied by a large collection for Edinburgh, namely 28 crates containing 88 birds of 34 varieties and 33 mammals of 19 varieties – and in addition two bags of sawdust, one bag of hay, and five bags of food including about 400 bananas. The crates were housed on the hospital deck (luckily not otherwise required), and almost every day I spent up to eight hours just cleaning the cages and feeding the animals and birds. Sailing time, the War being over, was back to normal, and after the usual 12 days I was glad to arrive at Southampton and be met by McPherson from Edinburgh Zoo who took over from me. It had been a tough voyage.

Having served for a full 18 months, I enjoyed 18 weeks at home. Then, in December 1947, with Elma and our two girls, we sailed back on the *Accra*. On board were Sir Gerald and Lady Creasy. He was to take over from Sir Alan Burns as Governor – and unluckily to find the pleasant and happy Gold Coast smitten by strikes, riots and all manner of disturbances (of which more later).

CHAPTER II

Tenth Tour:
January 1948 – April 1949

On arrival in the Gold Coast, there was another job for me. Government had recently created a new post of Judicial Adviser (to which I was soon to be promoted), to 'supervise' Native Courts generally. Already one had been appointed, my great friend A.J. Loveridge, and I was to work with him – supervising some 80 to 100 Native Courts throughout the Colony (which included southern Togoland, but excluded Ashanti and the Northern Territories).

I was stationed in Cape Coast (well known to me), where they had just built a new Government Lodge to go with the newly created post of Chief Commissioner, Colony – to balance Chief Commissioner, Ashanti. But after only two months of working in my new position, the whole of the Gold Coast became disturbed by disorder. I will not go into the history of this. It is well documented. But it began in Accra. On 28th February ex-servicemen, determined on marching to the Castle, refused to stop. The Police had to open fire. The trouble spread. At first it was only in Accra but soon it affected other places and even Kumasi, which had seemed likely to escape. In Cape Coast we were able to contain the trouble and after a few days my diary reports golf and snooker as usual (after, I may say, fairly continuous and strenuous work trying to keep the peace in Cape Coast and vicinity). But the troubles continued on and off for months. My diary jottings include:- "Nigeria troops . . . Koforidua chaotic . . . Cape Coast stores closed . . . boycott of imported goods . . . 22 deaths Accra . . . 2 sloops being sent to West Africa . . . censorship of the Press."

All this is just what the Press like and the reports in the UK newspapers were sensational. In Cape Coast it was worrying for a while but by early March (that is, only a week after it began) my diary records, "office as usual," and even treks to various places near Cape Coast. Then, on 15th March, rioting began in Kumasi, where we had been assured nothing would happen. It was this general ignorance of what was going on that forced us to start a Special Branch of the Police (a sort of MI5, which hitherto we had never needed). However with the promise of 'Inquiries,' etc., etc., peace was restored – though this was really the beginning of the demands for 'Independence' and the cry for 'Self-Government,' and hastened the day in 1957 when the Gold Coast would be the first colony in Tropical Africa to be granted its independence. Gold Coast troops had defeated the Italians in Somaliland. India had acquired Independence. Why not the Gold Coast?

However, by June I was again working normally, and travelling around inspecting Head Chiefs' Native Courts. I motored 600 miles in six days and inspected numerous Courts. It was work I enjoyed. These were not punitive inspections but rather helpful ones, giving guidance both to the Court Clerks as well as to the Chiefs and Elders in the keeping of records. On my return we (the four of us) moved to a better bungalow. I noted that on the day we moved, we actually had a dinner party that night for nine – which confirms what I wrote earlier about the remarkable efficiency of our servants (both steward boys and cook), and also our 'acceptance' of moving house.

One day – it was a Bank Holiday – we all went to nearby Saltpond to have lunch on the beach and then a swim. When I emerged from the sea, I found that my shorts, with a gold watch in the pocket, were missing. I went straight to the police, and then (probably their doing) "gong-gong" was beaten in the surrounding villages. This is a tribal custom, and an excellent one, by which the Chief imparts information (and invites response if necessary). I have no further details, other than to say that my clothes and gold watch were, an hour later, back in my safe keeping. However it happened, I was able to congratulate the Saltpond police on such a prompt recovery.

Later that month and in the following months I was continually on trek, inspecting numerous courts all over the Colony and Togoland. It was bad luck for Elma – but she had the children and a useful nanny, and the District Commissioners and other senior officers were all close friends, so she would not be lonely. From Cape Coast I nipped up to Kumasi one evening for the Ashanti Dining Club. As I had begun it, I wanted to maintain my links with it. A few months later I was a guest at the Accra Dining Club. 31 of us were there. It was too many and not nearly as intimate as the Ashanti Club. One day I noted in my diary that Kobina Sekyi came to tea with me. This was a real triumph for Sekyi was, and always had been, anti-British. He was a leading lawyer, had his own political party, and had fought for Independence for many years, but being an originator, was unwilling to assist other parties. In Cape Coast, several years earlier, he had refused to come to my house. So that day I was delighted with his visit.

In our vegetable garden in Cape Coast I planted cabbages, cauliflower, carrots, and both French and runner beans. Potatoes could be grown, but the result was negligible and the return was even less with green peas – I reckoned one pea per pea planted. The reason was that although we had ample heat and rain, there was not enough sunlight, the green pea needing say 15–16 hours daily but the Gold Coast, being near the equator, could give them only 12 hours. which was not enough.

One day I was in Kibbi and while there visited the Secondary School. This is worth a mention since the headmaster was William Ofori-Atta. He was a close relative of the Paramount Chief, Nana Sir Ofori Atta, the most powerful Head Chief in the Colony and in the Gold Coast as a whole second only to the Asantehene. William Ofori-Atta's Assistant was Kojo Botsio. These two, Willie Ofori-Atta and Kojo Botsio, were some four years later to become Cabinet Ministers – and I, indeed, became Botsio's Permanent Secretary. But at the time of my visit, while the school had an excellent reputation, it was also running at a huge loss and was seriously in debt – and William Ofori-Atta and Kojo Botsio were, not surprisingly, in great disfavour with the government.

My Christmas present that year from Elma was a set of Bannerman, the great naturalist who was compiling the massive seven volume *Birds of West Africa*. From that day I would use the book almost daily, and occasionally I wrote articles for the *Nigerian Field*. Once I had the privilege of meeting Mr Bannerman in the Kensington Museum, where he was engaged in a similar project for the birds of Britain.

Early in the next year, 1949, a lady who had kept many monkeys for some years was going away and offered them all to me, so I drove to Sekondi and returned with the nine monkeys. I put them in a large aviary or monkey house. Then, three days later, I went on one of my customary treks. When some 50 miles north of Cape Coast, I was stopped by a policeman who asked me to telephone Elma at home in Cape Coast. I did so. "The monkeys have escaped, would I come back quickly?" she said. But I could not, for I had a full four days' work ahead of me. I asked her to try to tempt them with food. Luckily these nine monkeys had been in confinement, really as pets, for some months, and Elma (and the keepers), with quantities of bananas and other tempting morsels, managed to persuade all nine back to their cage – a quite remarkable piece of animal handling.

Soon after this I had to prepare another consignment for Edinburgh Zoo. This would include a baboon. Hear of it:- a week earlier Kwasi had reported to me excitedly, on returning from the market where he had been buying the daily bone for soup for lunch, that he had seen a large baboon at the police station. He had enquired about it. It had been biting people and the owner, who did not want to kill it, was under arrest. But who would take it? So, off I went to the police station and was offered free this large baboon. It was tame at times, but could be rough. It sat in the car peacefully enough while I drove home. There I gave him a good sized kennel with a long length of chain (yes, chain, for a leather leash would have been useless), so that if he wished he could be out of the sun by day or the cold at night. I had him for about a week, and then heard of a boat sailing the next day. There was no worry until just when I was due to proceed to Takoradi. At that point baboon refused to enter his kennel – which was to become his travelling box. Each time I tried to coax him in, he made at me. It took the keeper and me fully an hour to inveigle him in, but in due course he went, with many more birds and mammals, to Edinburgh Zoo. There, Mr Gillespie later told me my baboon was put with others in a large open air enclosure, from which, however, five or six of them would regularly escape. They could not find out how. So one day three keepers stayed around a bit and then one hid and the other two very obviously withdrew. My baboon came out, looked around, peered every-where, saw the land was clear, no keepers in sight, and by a peculiar route led all the others to escape. I was glad to hear this tale of my primate friend.

In February we had Yaw Adu to stay. He and Kofi Busia (afore mentioned) were the first two Africans in the Gold Coast (perhaps in Africa?) to be appointed District Commissioners. This was the work of Sir Alan Burns – he believed in getting there first, before there was an outcry in the press or by politicians for Africans to be made DCs. Burns got in first. It was a gamble, but it worked. Adu was quite exceptional. At one time he had an important office in London, and many of us hoped he would become Commonwealth Secretary. But that did not happen and alas, he was offered a Directorship on Consolidated African Selection Trust which operated the large diamond open cast minefields in the Gold Coast. It was a great honour, the first Gold Coast African to be on the board of a British company, but many of us felt he could have climbed higher.

The following figures on school fees are interesting. The Ghana College in Cape Coast had 200 pupils, of whom 40 were boarders. Staff was eight masters each paid £120 p.a., and profit on the school was nearly £1,000 in one year. Soon after, I also visited Prempeh College in Kumasi, an excellent secondary school. They had 100 pupils, and for staff – a headmaster and six masters. Fees, for boarders, were £43 p.a. (plus textbooks). I wonder what the fees are today, and how much masters are paid?

At the end of March 1949 Elder Dempster telephoned. "*Tamale* will take zoo tomorrow." Luckily cargo ships were not all that prompt. I was able hurriedly to summon carpenters and hastily make crates, and so two days later I despatched to the shipping line 9 crates containing 13 monkeys, 2 baboons, and geese, together with four boxes of food and three bags of sawdust. And then, after a tour of 15 months, the five of us – Elma, the three children, and myself – and the livestock we had not been able to send on the *Tamale* – some 20 animals and bird boxes – all sailed on the *Tarkwa*. Tending this lot was much less work than the last time, a mere hour in the morning and the same in the evening. On the trip, however, at breakfast one morning, a steward approached me. "Sir," he said, "the monkeys are out." Somehow nine monkeys had escaped from their enclosure and were all over the ship's rigging. What fun! And I think the passengers also enjoyed it. Surprisingly, after less than an hour all nine had been persuaded, by dint of many bananas, to return to their temporary home.

After the usual 12 or 13 days we were landed at Liverpool. It was too late for the evening train to Edinburgh, so we dined at the Adelphi and caught a train at 1 a.m. (Elma having to tend our three young daughters). We reached Carstairs at 7 a.m., changed trains, and arrived in Edinburgh at 8 a.m. How glad we all must have been to arrive and be met by family! Hitherto we had either rented a house in Fife from my Aunt Madeline or stayed with my or Elma's parents. But this time I bought a house in Edinburgh for our own use on leave and to be let while we were abroad. We did this in August, 1949.

By now we were usually expected to travel by air rather than by sea, thus losing the twelve days' holiday we were used to on the boat. But so it was to be. This time, I was due to visit Sierra Leone to try some peculiar case up-country. I flew the usual London-Lisbon-Dakar route and, Freetown being too wet for the plane to land, spent three days in Dakar. Then on to Freetown, where I was met by my sister Margaret and her husband Hugh, a District Commissioner in Sierra Leone. I had a pleasant holiday with them, then heard the Native Court case I had come for and spent a few more days with Margaret in Bonthe, a delightful island where Hugh was DCI Then I flew on to Accra on 8th October, and thence back to Ashanti.

CHAPTER 12

Eleventh Tour:
October 1949 – February 1951

I was posted back to Kumasi. A month later Elma and the three girls arrived off the *Apapa* and we were very happy there. One day at a garden party given by the Asantehene, I met Lady Baden-Powell, who was visiting the Gold Coast Girl Guides. Two days later I was flying from Kumasi to Accra via Takoradi and as the plane flew low over Cape Coast, I approached Lady Baden-Powell and said, "If you look down there, you will see a large white building. That is Cape Coast Castle where your husband was stationed ere he led the advance party (actually called Scouts) on the British advance to and occupation of Kumasi in 1896."

I was Judicial Adviser, Ashanti, and one day I had inspected six Native Courts. A few weeks later, however, we were again on the move. In May 1950 I was posted back to Cape Coast, where I acted as Senior Judicial Adviser, having the supervision of some 150 Native Courts in the Colony. I had the power to correct any judgment I considered totally incorrect, and every clerk of court had to pass a test set by me. This was quite onerous, but being legally qualified, I enjoyed both the work and the travelling, which enabled me to see much of the Gold Coast. Now, in 1950, twenty-one years since I first landed in the Gold Coast, I was becoming one of the more senior DCs, so when the Chief Commissioner, Colony, my friend Commander T. R. O. Mangin, went to Accra for a short time as Acting Governor, I acted as Chief Commissioner, much to my enjoyment even though only for a fortnight.

In August I was promoted from Judicial Adviser to Senior Judicial Adviser. It is worthy of note that we still belonged to a powerful Colonial Service, for I received a letter signed by the Colonial Secretary, that "the Secretary of State had agreed to my promotion." A few months later, in November 1950, as Senior Judicial Adviser, I visited Togoland. One day, returning to Accra, I had a puncture and was running late. I saw a powerful African with a stout belt around his middle. I stopped him and enquired if he was a linesman. He answered that he was, so I asked him to shin up the nearest pole and put me through to my host in Accra. This was duly done – to my satisfaction, though the telephonist in Accra was rather cross with me for so incorrectly using the system. While on telephones, I am reminded of a Kumasi tale. There, in charge of the telephone girls, was a delightful Highland lady I'll call Miss M. One day the Chief Commissioner, Ashanti, was trying to talk to his opposite number in Tamale, 240 miles to the north. The line was bad and they could not hear each other. One of them remarked, "There is someone listening in," only to hear, "There's naebody listening in".

After my visit to Togoland it was back to Cape Coast. My diary tells me I played golf with J. S. Lawson, another DC who, on retiring, settled in St Andrews and became Captain, Royal and Ancient, St Andrews'. Soon after, having done some really extensive trekking, I sailed on the *Apapa*, reaching Liverpool late in February 1951. There I was met by Elma, and then driven in our car to our own home in Edinburgh. Maintaining my interest in ornithology, I spent a wonderful and ever to be remembered week in May in Fair Island (north of Orkney) with a dozen others, watching, counting, and ringing birds on migration.

In July, 1951, all five of us sailed on the *Apapa*, Elma with two daughters in one cabin, and I in another with Margaret, the eldest. At Freetown my sister and her husband came aboard, joined us for breakfast, and then took us ashore for a swim on Lumley Beach.

CHAPTER 13

Twelfth Tour:
July 1951 – October 1952

On landing at Takoradi, we drove to Cape Coast. I worked there as Senior Judicial Adviser for four months, and then was moved to Accra. The day after our arrival there we attended a garden party at Government House. There were 1,300 guests, rather a frightening number. My diary for this tour often merely records, "office daily – to 5 p.m." This was late for the Gold Coast, where we tried to work till 4 and then exercise from 4.30 to 6.

For a time I worked for Dr Kwame Nkrumah. I had several months as his secretary and we got on well. He had complete trust in me, but the work was rather dull for he was interested mostly in his political party, the Convention People's Party, and the struggle for 'Independence' or 'Self-Government,' – 'SG' as it was more commonly called for short. I remember once going to a political rally in Cape Coast where I heard Dr Busia bravely say, "We will be entitled to SG when our telephonists are able to answer a call properly and our policemen in the towns are able to direct traffic." Brave words! And while Nkrumah's party was crying, "SG now," Busia cried "SG next year." He had not a hope. At that meeting I remember a University Lecturer (actually, a Professor) speaking, "Don't listen to Government officers, they are only trying to slow things down. Don't listen to them, listen to us, we at the University are your friends." I thought this a very disloyal speech, so I was interested to learn that, a few years later, at the end of a student's oral examination for his degree, he asked the chairman if he might put a question to one of the professors. The chairman said that this was very unusual but he permitted it. The student then asked the professor if he would be so good as to say where he had obtained his Master of Arts degree. I believe this 'professor' left the Gold Coast by air the next day – he was a 'professor' who had never taken the degree he claimed.

Another story of Accra. One day I went to the Government Cattle Farm at Nungwa to see their efforts to breed better dairy cattle – for many Gold Coast cattle only gave 100 gallons a year, against say 1,000 gallons in the United Kingdom. But what interested me was the night watchman with a sling. It was the first and only time I have seen a sling in use. We all know the story of David and Goliath, and while believing it, I have often wondered at David's accuracy and the power of a stone to kill. I am no longer surprised. We had the watchman display his skill. The speed at which the stone left the sling was truly alarming. He buzzed it along the ground. Both speed and sound were frightening. I do not wonder that there was never a burglary there.

But speaking of burglaries – I have said I never lost anything while in the Gold Coast, that is, our boys (or servants) made sure no one ever robbed us. But I was burgled twice if not thrice in Accra. One particular time we were living in a standard-type government built house on stilts, four rooms and a closed verandah, in the centre a dining room and sitting room, and at each end a bedroom with its own bathroom. One night Elma and I woke up hearing some slight noise and thinking it was one of our three girls. I called out, "Come on darling, don't be frightened, come on darling." But as no daughter appeared, I rose up and went next door, to find a burglar wandering around. All he had taken was a pair of binoculars, no doubt thinking that the case held a camera. He was practically naked and well covered in oil. He was too quick for me. I failed to catch him, but if I had, I could never have held him on account of his protective grease or oil covering.

Wherever I worked it was strenuous. I loved being in a District, where one made one's own hours, but here in Accra, as my diary records, I worked frequently till 6 or 7 p.m., and one day from 2 to 11.30 p.m., Elma bringing me supper in the office. A few days later, after a full eight hours in the office, I see that I spent another three hours there after dinner. But as usual, there were compensations – no polo this time, but plenty of golf. I played once with Judge Korsah, soon to become Chief Justice of the Gold Coast and, in 1957, of Ghana. And there was bathing every Sunday, but no club life, so no bridge, chess or snooker, which was probably just as well with Elma and three children at home!

When the African Ministers first came to power, they were suspicious of the ('white') government from which they were taking over. They thought they could do better. One problem was the 'Shokbeton' housing scheme. This was sponsored by a Dutch firm, and the go-between was a well-known character, Eddie Chapman. He had been dismissed from the army before the war, acted in Germany as a spy, and then came to the UK and acted as a spy for the British – that is, he double-crossed the Germans. But his record was not savoury. (I have his book, *Free Agent*, where all this is set out). Once, sitting at Accra airport, Eddie Chapman was at the next table, and I remember Elma's excitement at sitting next to such a notorious (ex-)criminal. Anyhow, Dr Nkrumah and his politicians were keen to support this huge housing scheme, with new types of houses to be built all over the Gold Coast. We, the civil servants, were unable to act since we knew no details and the Cabinet was now almost entirely African – there were only three whites in it, in Defence, Treasury and Law. Everyone was very worried but I happened to be working with Nkrumah and so one day I asked if I might see the Shokbeton papers. He replied, "Of course," and gave them to me. I hurriedly had them copied and returned them to Nkrumah next morning. At this time we also used to examine or empty Nkrumah's waste paper basket daily – and search it. Now, this was not disloyalty but it exemplified a problem that was emerging. Hitherto the loyalty of the Civil Service was unquestionably to the Governor of the Gold Coast (and, of course, ultimately to the King). But now, with Nkrumah as Prime Minister, we also owed a loyalty to him and his Government. Once we found out about Shokbeton, we could formally discuss the problem with Nkrumah and, once he had heard and considered our views, then we would obey his decision. The problem in Accra was not acute, but I was to find that it became increasingly acute at a later date. The fact was that all Chief, Provincial, and District Commissioners also had a loyalty to the people amongst whom they worked. When I took charge of Ashanti – and this we shall come to below – there was a conflict between the Ashantis on the one hand, and Nkrumah and the Governor on the other. I could advise the Ashantis (that is, the Asantehene) on what I thought their best interests, but as regards actual obedience, there was no doubt about it: I had to obey Nkrumah.

Apart from being Permanent Secretary to the Ministry of Defence, and at another time to Prime Minister Nkrumah, I was also for a time at Government House as Secretary to the Governor. However, all this came to an end when I was promoted and appointed to the senior post in

South Togoland Council (with Mrs Russell and Self)

Togoland – that of Regional Officer, Togoland. The post was created in June, 1952, and I was the first to hold it, but only temporarily while the first substantive holder was on leave. After six weeks I was again back in Cape Coast, and on 20th July, when my great friend, A. J. Loveridge, went on leave, I stood in for him in the newly created post of Chief Regional Officer, Colony (formerly Chief Commissioner, Colony).

By this time Governor Creasy had been replaced by Sir Charles Arden-Clarke, a powerful man with strong views, capable of handling riots and any other trouble. And, as he had married a cousin of mine, Elma and I and the children were often invited to the Castle. Later on, when I was in Ashanti, and – like many Administrative Officers – did not always see eye to eye with the Governor, he was always more than kind in none the less having me to stay or be entertained at the Castle. One day I was delighted to return the compliment, when HE and his family came to Cape Coast and I was able to entertain them in the recently built Government Lodge.

Government Lodge, Cape Coast, with Mrs. Russell

In September, Elma and the children went on leave on the MV *Accra*. One day I went to Dodowa, to meet and address the Joint Provincial Council of Chiefs, which corresponded to the Asanteman Council but was much larger. It included Head Chiefs from all over the Colony (among them three who had been knighted, Sir Nana Ofori Atta, of the largest state in the Colony, Akim Abuakwa; Sir Emmanuel Mate Kole, of the Krobos in the Eastern Province; and Sir Tsibu Darku, of Asin Attandaso near Cape Coast). The following night Sir Tsibu Darku came to dine with me – and a great pleasure it was. But the real excitement, while I was Acting Chief Regional Officer and living in the well-appointed Government Lodge in Cape Coast, was the visit of the Prime Minister, Dr Kwame Nkrumah. I was not surprised. He had not previously stayed with any European official, but I had been his secretary, and though he knew that my views on Self-Government, on Ashanti, and on a few other matters were not in agreement with his, he also knew that I could be trusted. I was delighted at the prospect. He duly arrived one evening at 7 p.m., in a car with a driver but no one else – this when Europeans never travelled without a servant, to carry the luggage, unpack, run the bath, etc., etc. However, this did not inconvenience me, as there were ample servants at Government Lodge. According to custom, I naturally offered Nkrumah a drink. This is a story I often tell. "Yes," he said. "Whisky?" – no. "Gin?" – no. "Then maybe a soft drink?" "Yes," he said. And I added, "With a little rum in it?" "Yes," he answered. Make of this what you will!

In the evening I had a small dinner party for Nkrumah. It included an Archbishop, a Roman Catholic Vicar-General, Sir Tsibu Darku, three Members of the Legislative Assembly, and four District Commissioners – twelve of us in all, and a happy evening it was. I had of course sent the draft list to the Prime Minister for his approval, and he had agreed to all except the Archbishop. I replied that he could not be omitted and in due course Nkrumah agreed. But next morning, driving with him (actually in my car, with the orderly in front, and flying as usual the Union Jack on the bonnet), he asked me if I knew why he had not wanted the Archbishop included. I said that I had no idea. The Prime Minister replied, "Really rather silly. When, many years ago, I was teaching in Accra, before leaving for America I asked for a loan of a term's salary, £30, and he gave me this. I have never repaid it yet."

In the morning I took Nkrumah to see as much as we could in the time available. We had broken fast at 7 a.m., and at 8 left on a four hours' inspection: to Elmina – the Castle, police station, prison, leprosarium; then back to Cape Coast – Wesley Girls High School, Adisadel College (Anglican), a housing estate, the Roman Catholic press; then to my office to meet the District Commissioners. I then gave the Prime Minister lunch, after which we left for Saltpond – a short inspection there – and then Swedru. At 5 p.m. the PM continued to Accra, and I to Koforidua, and the following day up North to open new District Council Offices, followed by a drinks party at noon for 40 – fully half of whom were African.

And then came the time for leave once again. Instead of the usual formal handing over of a District, one DC to the next DC, I went in to Accra, met my friend Johnny Loveridge at the Accra Airport, handed 'the Colony' back to him, and boarded my plane for the UK. Now, 1952, in there was a new route, via Kano (Northern Nigeria) and Tripoli, to London.

Early in January 1953, it was time to return to work. On 7th January I went south and spent a night on board HMS *Theseus*, which was commanded by my brother Douglas (then a Captain). On the 9th I flew from London in the afternoon, reached Tripoli in the evening, then on to Kano, and Accra by 10 a.m. Believe it or not, my diary records me as being in the office by 11 a.m.

CHAPTER 14

Thirteenth Tour:
January 1953 – May 1954

"In my office by 11 a.m." The office in question was that of the Ministry of Education and Social Welfare. I had again been promoted and was to be Permanent Secretary under Mr Kojo Botsio, the (Cabinet) Minister for Education – and to be in that position for the whole tour of 16 months. I had been going back to a rural posting, but my predecessor, Mr Thomas Barton, an able Scot and former Director of Education, had died, so I was rushed in to take his post. It was not easy because, as you may remember from above, I had met Mr Botsio and Mr Ofori Atta at their school in Kibbi, a good school but one hopelessly in debt, and somewhere Mr Barton had minuted, when Mr Botsio had applied for promotion, "He is not fit even to be a junior Education Officer." It was rumoured that Mr Botsio, now Minister for Education, had had a sight of this minute! I did not have an easy time but Mr Barton might have had an even more difficult one.

Yes, it was far from easy. Once I was having a dinner party, and sent in to Botsio a note saying, "I am having to dinner the Directors of Education of Nigeria, Sierra Leone, the Gambia, and our own – it would be a pleasure etc., etc., if you would join us." And I had the reply in writing, "No fraternisation before Independence." Our work relationship was reasonable but social – nil, even though I was having many Africans to my house, attending the Prime Minister's parties, and the like.

In this Ministry there were just two Departments – Education and Social Welfare, but we were associated with no less than 27 Boards. Education was Jack Marshall – an able man: he began at Achimota, and was both a good rugger player (who had played for Oxford Greyhounds) and a good ornithologist. The Director of Social Welfare was an African, Robert Gardiner, the first African to head a Department, also able and most likeable. All Europeans respected him as a civil servant and as a person. One morning he brought in to me a wee scrap of paper he had found on his desk: – "Scholarships to be given to . . .", and there followed some six or seven names of African pupils. What was he to do? I don't say the note was from Botsio but we wondered. I, or any other European, would just laugh and tear up the note. Our homes were in Britain and our pensions guaranteed by the Crown Agents. But how different for Gardiner. The Civil Service was now entirely under African control. If anyone misbehaved or annoyed a Minister, they could promptly be sacked. In this particular case I said that I would deal with it. As far as I remember, I believe I handed the note to Botsio and asked him if he knew where it came from.

I am led here to say a brief word on *corruption*. This is the headache of Africa today, and indeed of many other countries. In my time in the Gold Coast, when anyone paid, say, 10s. for a gun licence, he would automatically, by native custom, be expected to say "thank you" by giving the clerk 2s. It was all most courteous, and a quite delightful habit. But, if the person failed to say "thank you," or appeared unlikely to do so, the clerk might withhold the licence till he received his 2s. Here was a subtle but very real difference. One day the police had good evidence of a clerk demanding the 2s. ere giving the licence. The clerk, to our delight, was duly prosecuted. But the District Magistrate (an ex-Naval officer, no less) discharged him, saying that it was just Native Custom. We were back at square one and corruption continued to escalate.

In many matters I found myself fully on Botsio's side and especially in dealings with the University and its prickly Principal, David Balme. Balme was insisting on 'academic freedom' to absurd lengths. Everyone recognises that there must be academic freedom but in a new university entirely dependent on Government funding, all that Botsio wanted – and I agreed – was that the University should give considerable emphasis to the needs of the country, that is, to medicine, law, engineering, agriculture, forestry, and the like. But Balme wished it to be a 'complete' University, with a full quota of faculties. We also had considerable disputes over the lengths of the University's tours. The University wished for all the staff to be on site for 8–9 months, then all to have an annual leave of 7–8 weeks in the long vacation. Botsio said that this was too expensive, and that leave should only be after 19 months. I left it to them to decide. I had begun on 18 months tours, but we were just about to change, flying having become the norm, to 9 months tours and short leaves. But I do remember at one of these sessions, when Botsio had been pleading for 18 months tours, a professor, a Scot, saying uncompromisingly, "Minister, you can come back here as often as you wish – and we will always give you the same answer."

I might mention a very clever scheme, run by Britain and London University, as new universities were springing up all over the Colonial Empire. Each foundation was to be (originally, when Britain still had a say), a 'College' of London University, so that degrees granted by the university in Accra were thus of equal standing with those of London University itself. This took a lot of double marking and checking of examination papers, involving external examiners, but it was well worth while.

One school of which the Gold Coast was very proud was Achimota, begun by Rev. A. G. Fraser, a Scot, who came to Accra from Kandy College, Ceylon, accompanied by Mr A. H. R. Joseph, a (Ceylonese) games master. Fraser was supported enthusiastically by Guggisberg, Governor of the Gold Coast in the 1920s. Fraser's motto or badge for Achimota was the keys of the piano – white are of no use without black and vice versa. Both are needed. Fraser built Achimota on the lines of an English Public School and, to help, appointed as staff many Oxford graduates. The whole project was astoundingly successful. But one day, after a long vacancy, no one could decide on who was to be the next Headmaster. So the Cabinet made an appointment. Naturally I heard about this. That evening, as so often, I was walking in the Achimota woods listening to and watching birds and I was accompanied by my friend, J. R. Marshall (an Achimotan ere he became Director of Education). When I told him about the appointment, he was so distressed, said it was impossible and gave me reasons for his views. I had known Marshall for over 20 years, and had total confidence in his opinion. His views strongly influenced mine. Next morning I told Botsio my views, and asked if I might see the Prime Minister. Botsio agreed so over I went and told the PM what I thought. Nkrumah asked, "Can the man we want not do it?" "Yes," I replied, "but Achimota will no longer be the best school in tropical Africa." Nkrumah asked me what I recommended. I said that we had just heard of a suitable candidate. "Right," said Nkrumah; "go up to the Castle, ask the Governor to send him a cable offering him the appointment, and I will tell the Cabinet they have made a mistake." I tell this to show how Cabinet Ministers, who were now running the country, knew that the Europeans (or at least most of them) had the best interests of the Gold Coast at heart. But while I disliked so much of what Nkrumah was doing – for example, fighting for Self-Government too soon – yet it was pleasing to be so trusted.

Among my many friends at the University was Professor A. W. Lawrence, brother of Lawrence of Arabia, and he and I often met either in his house or mine. Alas, I found the Principal, Dr David Balme, very difficult. I have mentioned already his extreme insistence on academic independence (and it was extreme). However, twice I was a great help to him. Once was when he wanted the Government to enact some special regulations for the University and Botsio (or Nkrumah) objected. Advised by the Attorney General, I was able to tell Balme that he could enact what he wanted under his own bye-laws. The second occasion was when Balme wanted extra land for a Botanic Garden, a farm, possibly a zoo, etc., etc. He asked for some 5 to 10 acres. In the paper I submitted to the Cabinet I suggested, if I remember rightly, about some 400 acres just north of Accra in a vast uncultivated stretch of land. The Cabinet agreed without a murmur. In neither case did Balme say a word of thanks.

I have mentioned earlier how the Gold Coast University was classified as part of London University, so that its degree was of similar standard. I encountered and helped to operate a similar device at a lower level. The Chief Executive of the West African Examinations Council lived in Accra, and so I was in constant touch with him. His job involved the external examining of School Leaving Certificates, so that all Secondary Schools in the Gold Coast, Nigeria, and (I think) Sierra Leone, had the same worth.

I have reported burglaries in Accra. During this tour I was burgled no less than three times, in February, April, and December. My house was not only mosquito-proofed but it was also supposedly 'burglar-proofed.' Actually burglars never entered the house on these three occasions. Between the outside proofing and the sitting room and bedrooms, there ran a narrow passage (frequent in the tropics for the sake of temperature), and the burglar would poke a long walking stick through the gauze and unhook from the coat rack a pair of binoculars in the mistaken belief that he was getting a camera. I actually lost two pairs of binoculars this way.

One week we had a petrol strike, which I mention to show how different life was in Accra from North-West Ashanti. It meant that for a week I walked to the office and back, good exercise but unpleasant if one was neatly dressed in a suit and wearing a tie. It was about this time, outside my work, that I found myself assuming responsibilities in other spheres.

I became Chairman of the Accra branch of the Nigerian Field Society (in the magazine of which I occasionally wrote articles on collecting for a zoo, or on some particular birds I had seen). In 1953 I acted as Chairman of the Management Committee of the Ridge Church, and the next year was elected substantive Chairman. I used to worship there when in Accra. It had been established for Europeans but there was, of course, no colour bar and several Africans worshipped with us. It had two Anglican, one Presbyterian, and one Methodist service monthly, and on a fifth Sunday it might be the Salvation Army. I was also involved in the Legion – the British Legion but here known as the Gold Coast Legion, but more of this anon.

My wife and I enjoyed entertaining. While Permanent Secretary at the Ministry of Education, I gave several semi-official parties. I noted in my diary one of 30 folk including several Cabinet Ministers, but alas, not my own Minister, Botsio. And soon after, on Margaret's tenth birthday, Elma gave a party for 27 children – how different from 20 years ago when there were few white women and no white children! I also gave a tea party for senior office staff, eight white and twenty black.

It was now 1954. One day I attended the Legislative Council. It was to be the last time in which it included any Europeans or any Chiefs. All seats in future were after due elections (as in the UK). And so, after a tour of 16 months, we all sailed for home, all five of us. This was in May 1954. My diary tells me that the luggage we took with us was 15 pieces, while we left 80 pieces (luggage, crates, etc.) in storage. After four months in the house I had bought three years before, we left Margaret in boarding school, and with Elma and the two younger children we sailed on the *Aureol*, Elder Dempster's newest boat.

CHAPTER 15

Fourteenth Tour: October 1954 – July 1955

For the next ten months I was again stationed in Accra, not in a Ministry this time but as Secretary to the Governor. This did not entail living in the Castle, and we had an excellent bungalow in Accra. 'Expatriates' were getting fewer. Each time there was an amendment to the Gold Coast Constitution, our conditions of service would change, for basically we were now subject to an African Cabinet and not to the Governor. But we still had many perquisites, for example, travel to and fro for our children, so that though we had left Margaret at home in school, she was able, at government expense, to fly out and back. For Catherine's birthday party we were now up to 46. And in the Ridge Church I noted that the Sunday School held 70 children, mainly white.

In November there was the usual Remembrance Day parade and church service. For this the Governor took the salute. Many of us would be in white uniform. Perhaps Chris Patton was right to stop all this dressing up when he was appointed Governor of Hong Kong, but the African (at least in the Gold Coast) loved 'finery,' and themselves used enormous umbrellas, drums, horns, marvellous rich silk robes, and so forth. In attendance would be many officials, unofficials, ex-servicemen, and of course a Guard of Honour – a white officer and rank and file Africans, the latter largely Muslims. I suggested to the Governor, Arden-Clarke, that there should be fitted in somewhere a Mohammedan prayer, given by an African Sergeant or other Muslim. To this there was fierce opposition from the Anglican Bishop who would be taking the service. I'm glad that Arden-Clarke insisted, saying that if there was not, he would not himself attend. And I might mention that Arden-Clarke was an Anglican who attended church regularly.

The Ridge Church was booming, mainly white but with more and more Africans attending. I thought we should build a school for the white children but technically to be for all without reference to colour, race or religion.

The Ridge Church accepted my idea with enthusiasm. Unfortunately Judge (later Chief Justice) Korsah had had a similar idea. His was to be the International School. I sent out the appeal, and called on many people personally. When I called on the head of Unilever he replied, that I was just a week too late. Korsah had been in first, and Unilever had subscribed handsomely. But he was kind enough to give a personal donation. Eventually the school was built, and proved to be a great success. Indeed, I was invited to come to Accra from Kumasi to lay the Foundation Stone, and I was given a silver trowel which I proudly keep. This was in 1956. The school opened the next year with 33 children. The next year it had 100, and by 1967 no less than 300 – of 25 nationalities. The school has thrived – indeed it has, for at the time of going to press (1996) I learn that the roll is 1,150.

Another activity of mine, but small, was with the Gold Coast Legion. I was chairman of the Accra Branch, and when in 1955 a new Legion Hall was opened by the Governor, I was in the chair, and when we opened a Legion Village, again I chaired this and had the Prime Minister on my right and Brigadier Paley, commanding Gold Coast Troops, on my left. Elma was also kept very busy. Apart from having a large Sunday School, she ran the Brownies, and once paraded with 28 of them in church. Work was not too heavy, but sometimes I was still woken up late at night, and obliged to go to the Castle to work on deciphering some secret telegram. This did not happen often.

I must tell here a story that some of you may know. In about 1992, Channel 4 Television put on a series, 'End of Empire,' beginning with India and going on to all tropical Africa. For the Gold Coast section I appeared on the screen with this conversation:- "I was Secretary to the Governor, Sir Charles Arden-Clarke, and one day I heard in the room next to mine nothing but, 'I can't hear you,' repeated time and time again." I then said that after the Gold Coast riots in 1948, Arden-Clarke was sent to calm the country. He was a powerful individual, who had begun his overseas career in Northern Nigeria, where he might not see another European for six months or even a year. He liked taking decisions. When the telephone receiver was put down, Sir Charles came into my office. "I can't hear you, I can't hear you" – I was puzzled. "That," he said, "was the Secretary of State. I can accept despatches and even cables – but I am not going to have him telephoning me." Life in 1995 would not have suited him, when Prime Ministers and Presidents regularly chat to each other and

Ambassadors seem to be by-passed. When Sir Charles went on leave, my friend Gordon Hadow, who was Deputy Governor, acted as Officer Administering the Government, and when he went on trek I was gazetted (admittedly for only a short time) as Officer Administering the Government.

After a ten months tour (which was becoming the practice, followed by a short leave of ten weeks), I flew home, Elma and the girls having preceded me by sea. We spent part of our leave again at Kintail – where I spent nearly all my time climbing the numerous 'Munros' in the vicinity. And then, after two months leave, on 30th September 1955, leaving the two elder girls at school, Elma and I with our youngest daughter, Bridget, returned to the Gold Coast by air – the route then still being London-Rome-Tripoli-Kano. We arrived in Accra at noon the following morning.

CHAPTER 16

Fifteenth Tour:
October 1955 – July 1956

As was customary, one behaved as though one had not been absent, and on the evening of my return I chaired a meeting of the Ridge Church Council. But, two days later, my work really began. It was what I had, over the foregoing 25 years, been trained for: to serve as Chief Commissioner, Ashanti.

We drove to Kumasi, where I was to act as, and was soon promoted to, Chief Commissioner, Ashanti – now re-styled Chief Regional Officer. I don't think I was ever overly ambitious. Once I did ask if I would ever be considered for promotion. I was told, bluntly, that Colonial Secretaries were being appointed at 45, so that Governors could be appointed at 50, thus giving them 15 years as Governor. And when I asked – well, I was

The Residency, Kumasi

already 45! But, if not ambitious, I certainly enjoyed promotion, and probably in my dreams had hoped that one day would end up as Chief Commissioner, Ashanti.

In the 1930s the Chief Commissioner (CCA) was second in seniority only to the Governor, but in the 1950s, with the establishment of Parliamentary Government, there were one or two officers in Accra now senior to the CCA Nevertheless, the CCA – or CRO – was still the senior Administrative Officer outside Accra. And I was really thrilled to be appointed. Let me describe the Residency. It was a large handsome house, set in a huge garden with a large Silk Cotton tree some 120 feet high. It had been planted by HRH Marie Louise, Duchess of Argyll, in 1924. In it the large fruit bats used to roost. One evening I counted them – 300 of them. But they were our friends. Like the geckoes (lizards) in the house, they consumed moths and insects that would otherwise have been a nuisance. There were many small beds of brightly coloured flowers, canna lilies and others. The grounds were some 25 acres in extent, and in a corner of it I planted 370 pineapples, 130 bananas, and 20 or 30 miscellaneous fruit trees. The grass was cut by ordinary machete or similar weapon – we could afford a few lawn mowers, but not enough. The house, modern, had had an extension built in 1925 called the 'Governor's Wing,' specially built for the Prince of Wales. The main entrance to the Residency was up an attractive private road, lined on both sides with Royal Palms and having the Quarter Guard of the Gold Coast Regiment stationed at the entrance. They turned out daily when I first passed on my way to the office, but at other times the sentry merely saluted. My personal staff consisted of a cook and two steward boys, and there was a government paid staff of 8: two caretakers, washman, nightwatchman and four others, in addition to a garden staff of 13.

Across the road was my main office, another handsome building. There was a large room for myself on the first floor, with a huge table in it for meetings. The next room was my secretary's, a District Commissioner, and at the other end was the Assistant CCA or CRO On the ground floor were some 20 clerks, telephonists, messengers, etc. The usual office hours were 8 a.m. to noon, and 2 p.m. to 4. I would be in the main office from 8 to 12, but in the afternoon I usually worked in my private office, which was below the Governor's bedroom. However, as up-country, I often preferred the six hours in one, that is, from 7 a.m. to 1 p.m., then a curry lunch,

Kumasi, C.A.A.'s Office, Self, 1956

and a sleep ere whatever recreation was afoot. Recreation could be golf or tennis or squash or gardening or bird watching. I was still collecting for Edinburgh Zoo and had aviaries at the side of the house. I often had four or five varieties of birds of prey, four or five different species of owl, and at times a huge eagle, a present from the Asantehene, (which, incidentally, lived in Edinburgh for many years).

My tasks, like that of a District Commissioner, were not closely defined. They were basically the same, except that the CCA was responsible for all Ashanti, with a population of about a million and an area of about 25,000 square miles (see Appendix II). In this area the CCA had to encourage the DCs to further Local Government, to assist the Asantehene and the Asanteman Council in their administration of Ashanti, and to try to minimise tribal disputes – and, generally, to be in touch with all departments (other than the judiciary) and to discuss and help them with their problems.

Looming over all was Self-Government. It was being hastened forward by Nkrumah and also by the Governor, Arden-Clarke, whose term of office had been extended beyond his five years to let him bring the Gold Coast to Independence. It was easily the first colony in Tropical Africa (British, French, Belgian or whatever) to be heading for immediate self-rule. Opposed to Nkrumah were most of the Ashanti, and they started a political party, the National Liberation Movement (NLM). The Convention People's Party (CPP), led by Nkrumah, was in a vast majority in the Colony, and this was quite likely a hang-over of fear from the Ashanti storming down and wrecking their lands. But the CPP was in a minority in Togoland, in the Northern Territories, and of course in Ashanti. With such a huge majority in the south, however, they had a large over-all majority and so plans for Independence went ahead.

Our main problem was the matter of loyalty. We had, as I mentioned earlier, a loyalty to the Governor and also to Nkrumah, but we also had a loyalty to those with whom we worked. For the last 25 years there was no conflict, but now there was. This problem applied to me and to all the District Commissioners. In practice I found, as I have said, that I acted on Nkrumah's orders but listened to and gave advice to the people where I worked, that is, the Asantehene and others. Actually, we succeeded. There were occasional murders but no real fighting. It was usually the NLM who would drive round Kumasi at night in a taxi, see a CPP man they did not like, drive round again and shoot. – frightening, occasionally wounding, rarely killing. Then they would change number plates and so no one was the wiser. Our Kumasi Police acted not unlike the Royal Ulster Constabulary in Northern Ireland – prosecuting people from whatever group, and acting efficiently, even though their sympathies undoubtedly lay in a certain direction. The shootings in Kumasi were rarely serious and were often not even reported to me, but they were given much publicity in the UK Press. My mother-in-law would write to us, very worried – were we safe and so on? I mention this just to show how the press can make a good story out of insignificant events.

Not immediately on my arrival, but later on, I used to have weekly meetings in my office of all Heads of Departments, including the local senior police officer and the senior Army officer (a Colonel in charge of the depot). Following such meetings, when I would receive information from as many people as possible, I would send a confidential report to the Governor, but not to Nkrumah. An example of such a report, dated 2nd

January 1957, will be found in Appendix VII. Nkrumah received his own reports from his henchmen in Kumasi.

One of my other tasks was 'socialising,' that is, giving hospitality to distinguished visitors. And they were non-stop. I arrived in Kumasi on 4th October, 1955, and the very next day I was entertaining an American Senator and his wife. I think I was generous, but I was expected to do some entertaining as I was in receipt of a large entertainment allowance. Only once did I emphatically refuse. The Prime Minister's Office phoned me one day: "Mr Bing is passing through Kumasi tomorrow and the PM would like you to give him lunch." "No," I replied. The message was repeated, and I gave the same answer. "Do you want me to tell the Prime Minister that?" I was asked. "Yes, if you wish," I replied. The person in question was a Queen's Counsel, and had also been a member of Parliament in the UK. It is said that he lost his seat and his wife in the same year! He was a 'special adviser' to Nkrumah, paid by him. I disliked him intensely. I had never met him, but I was determined not to have him in my house. I thought Nkrumah would be cross with me, indeed angry – but not disappointed. He would remember my insistence on the Archbishop being present in Cape Coast, and he knew well my interest in and love of the Gold Coast – even if my political opinions differed from his.

As the Gold Coast approached Independence, the number of visitors to the country, and to Kumasi, increased enormously. The following pages will be mainly 'social,' listing the many interesting visitors I was privileged to entertain in this period. I have referred earlier to the custom of "signing books," old fashioned but useful. In Kumasi a number of people signed my book every day. The names would be typed, and placed on my desk the next morning. I would then arrange, in the case of newcomers, how and when to entertain them, and from time to time I would check the lists to make sure that I had entertained all those whom I felt it my duty to have done so.

My first distinguished visitor was Sir Frederick Bourne, lately of the Indian Civil Service, but now in the Gold Coast to assess the Ashanti versus Brong situation. So the next night I had a dinner party for him – 14 of us, including the Asantehene, a Judge (African), and the Principal of the Kumasi College of Technology. Two days later, taking Sir Frederick Bourne with me, we left the Residency early in the morning, and reached Sunyani (80 miles) for breakfast. We had meetings with the Brongs and with the anti-Brongs, and returned to Kumasi by 4 p.m.. And remember, this was in the humid tropics where our roads were not like those at home, and where there were no fans or air conditioning in the cars. Sir Frederick, then in his 60s, must have felt it a long day.

A few days later I entertained Vice-Admiral Sir Ian Campbell, and had a dinner party of 16. A few days later I had Judge Quashie-Idun (African) to lunch. I should mention that at all dinners, even when I dined alone, we had no fan but a punkah which was pulled by my night-watchman who sat discreetly out of sight, lolling back in a chair, pulling the punkah with his toe – and keeping his bow and poisoned arrows lying beside him (though, needless to say, no one would dream of coming anywhere near the Residency at night, knowing that they might meet him).

Later in the month guests arrived continuously, filling all my three spare rooms. We would have drinks with the Asantehene, and then I would give a dinner for 14, of which half would be African. In December I had the Governor and his two daughters to stay, and a few days later I arranged for the Police Band to play at the Residency during a sherry party of some 64 guests. The next visitor to stay was Mr Edwards, General Manager of the Ashanti Goldfields.

My next visit to Accra included not only the usual meetings with the Prime Minister and the Governor, but I also met my elder daughters, who came out for the Easter holidays – and thanks to Sir Charles' kindness, all five of us were entertained at Government House for the night. Leaving early next morning, we had breakfast with a friend at Koforidua, and were in Kumasi (160 miles) in time for lunch. How different from the 1930s, when the road was scarcely motorable and the train journey took ten hours! The day after we arrived back in Kumasi, my eldest daughter's temperature was 104°, really rather high. I often used to reach 103°, but rarely 104°: this is on the danger mark.

My next guest was Lady Cripps, who came to lunch, and then soon after Lady Cripps again with her daughter Peggy, now married to Joe Appiah, a leading Ashanti barrister, and their eldest child, Kwame.

It was now 1956. Early in January I was elected president of the Kumasi Golf Club. But this was not surprising, for many honours, privileges, and also duties, were thrown on to the Chief Commissioner – or Regional Officer as we were now called. In return, there is no doubt that we were expected to appear publicly on numerous occasions, and also to entertain almost lavishly. While I had a magnificent time, work, social and recreation, yet work was at times distinctly strenuous. One day in 1956 I left Kumasi early, at 4.30 a.m., arrived in Accra for breakfast, had meetings as usual with the Governor and the Prime Minister and this time also with the Minister for Local Government, and left Accra at 7.30 that evening to reach Kumasi at midnight – a fairly full 20-hours day including 350 miles of motoring. A few days later I went out west, into Brong country, and held a uniform Durbar for 4– or 5,000 Domaas, then back to Sunyani for a sherry party of 25 in the evening. The next day I travelled to Accra (250 miles), including a meeting with the Asantehene as I passed through Kumasi. Then back to Kumasi the next day.

The next guest to stay was Sir Christopher Cox, and at dinner again Lady Cripps. When Cox departed, Sir George Seal of the Colonial Office arrived to stay, and for him I had a sherry party of some 70 guests with the Regimental Band playing on the Residency lawn. The following day a pleasant change, I enjoyed the hospitality of the Regimental Mess while their band beat retreat. But again, early next morning a quick visit to Accra to see the Governor at the airport as he left for the UK, and then back to Kumasi. Another 350 miles that day!

One evening my wife and I were invited to dine with the Kumasi Bar Association (all African) when they met to say farewell to one of the Ashanti judges (African). The following day this same judge was given a farewell service by the Kumasi Methodist Church. It was a Sunday and I attended. The service lasted over three hours – the normal services being one and a half to two hours.

Later that month, February 1956, I journeyed to Obuasi to stay with General Sir Edward Spears. He had recently taken over as General Manager of the Ashanti Goldfields. He was not an engineer and his position was somewhat resented by some of the senior mine staff, but it was a brilliant appointment. Spears was a politician and a tactician and had excellent relations with Dr Nkrumah – and this was fundamental. Before dinner Spears had said to me that he had an awkward customer coming to join us – a professor from the Accra University – and he would be glad of my help. So casually, after dinner, I asked the professor, "Have you many students in your faculty?" "Yes," he replied, "one or two," to which, rather rudely, I asked, "Which?" I received the embarrassing reply, "Well, as you ask, one." I give this as an example of the problem the Ghana Government

TABLE PLAN

Mr. J. Appiah

Mr. P. Boatin	Mr. J.W. Tsiboe
Mr. M.I.N. Gordon	Mrs. J.W. Caldow
Dr. W.E. Duncanson	Mr. R. Fort, M.P.
Mrs. J. Appiah	Nana Essumejahene
Rt. Hon. Creech Jones, M.P.	Lady Cripps
Mrs. A.C. Russell	His Honour
Otumfuo Asantehene	Mrs. W.E. Duncanson
Mr. W.W. Hamilton, M.P.	Lord Geddes
Mrs. R. Hughes	Mrs. J.W. Tsiboe
Mr. W.J. Caldow	Mr. R. Hughes

Secretary

Key (clockwise): Mr. J. Appiah: Barrister, Ashanti Bar. Mr. J. W. Tsiboe: founder and proprietor, *Ashanti Pioneer*. Nana Essumejahene: one of the most senior Head Chiefs of Asante. Lady Cripps: wife of Sir Stafford Cripps. Lord Geddes: member of the Parliamentary party. Mr. R. Hughes: Manager, Bank of British West Africa. Otumfuo Asantehene: Nana Sir Osei Agyeman Prempeh II. Rt. Hon. Creech Jones: formerly Secretary of State for the Colonies. Mrs. J. Appiah: formerly Miss Peggy Cripps. Dr. W. E. Duncanson: Principal, Kumase College of Technology (now University of Science and Technology, Kumasi). Mr. P. Boatin: Private Secretary to the Asantehene.

Seating plan for a dinner party given for M.P.'s prior to Independence was up against. The University wished to have a full quota of faculties and professors. The Ghana Government, which totally financed the University, wished it to show some economies, and to concentrate on law, medicine, agriculture, engineering and the like.

By the Spring, Ghana was rapidly approaching Independence, and was being swamped by VIPs, many of whom wished to visit Kumasi where the bulk of the opposition to Nkrumah lay. Thus, one day in mid-March Creech-Jones, then an eminent MP, arrived to stay, followed almost immediately by a large party of MPs – I think there were seven in all, headed by Lord Geddes. I had only four of them to stay, but on the 14th I gave a dinner party for 22, which included the Asantehene, the Essumajahene (about the second senior chief in Ashanti), Lady Cripps, her daughter Peggy and husband Joe Appiah, the Principal of the College of Technology, and the editor of the Kumasi newspaper and his wife (see Table Plan). My parties usually ended by 11 p.m., but this went on till well after midnight. I think the MPs were really delighted to meet such interesting and attractive Africans as those I had invited.

In spite of the late night, I met with the MPs in my office for an hour early next morning. Then I took them for another hour with the CPP (Nkrumah's party), then an hour with the Asantehene (and champagne), another hour with the NLM (Busia's opposition party), and so on to the Kumasi College of Technology where the Principal gave us lunch. I think I must have been quite relieved when the MPs continued their journey on that afternoon.

In April I gave another sherry party for 50, made another of my rapid day trips to Accra to see the Governor and Prime Minister, and sent off another consignment to Edinburgh Zoo. At the end of April (and this is less than twelve months ere Independence), I went to Bekwai, to the opening of a new water supply. Maybe a year earlier I would have been asked to open it, but now, with an entirely African Cabinet, it was natural that the Cabinet Minister responsible should perform. He, however, was a rabid CPP man, and Bekwai was staunchly NLM The Police provided 100 men, and trouble was avoided.

Other guests who came to stay included General Paley (commanding the Gold Coast Regiment), and Sir Robert Jackson (adviser to the Government on the Volta River project). Then the Governor himself came. After that Elma and I managed a visit to Kintampo. We met our old friend,

Sarikin Fanyinamah Wangara, and later I gave a sherry party for the Station (a term that means the senior officials and unofficials). Then another sherry party at Bekwai.

I mention in passing that the accepted way of corresponding with Chiefs was for us to address them as "My good friend" and end the letter in similar fashion – and they did the same when writing to the District Commissioner. This comes to mind, for a Chief living near Lake Bosumtwi wrote to me, "My dear Chum." I wish I had kept the letter.

July began with a CPP meeting in Kumasi. They had a large gathering in the spacious Prince of Wales Park. I visited the park almost hourly to see what trouble was happening. Actually my diary records, "preceded by 2 shootings; accompanied by 2 explosions, 1 shooting and 1 case of arson; and followed by an ambush causing 1 killed and 10 wounded." It might have been much worse!

Under local regulations, a passage was allowed to a wife once each way per tour, and the same for children – so the custom was for Elma to have the children out for one holiday and to be in Scotland for another, and maybe I could manage to be at home for it. Anyhow, early in July it was time for Elma and my youngest daughter to return to the UK for the summer holidays of the other two girls. So one night we travelled to Takoradi by the night train. There were no sleepers (as we know them) in Ghana, but the Traffic Manager kindly put his special coach at our disposal and so we travelled in great comfort. I saw Elma off by the *Aureol* in the afternoon, and then returned to Kumasi on the night train.

In spite of fairly continuous and heavy work and entertaining, I was still able to collect, house, and feed quite a number of birds and animals destined for Edinburgh. And I sent another consignment, this time only of birds, to Edinburgh Zoo.

In July I was to have another group of MPs and journalists descend on me, this time for the elections which were due to be held on the 17th of the month. The visitors were due at the Residency for lunch, but a bridge in the Northern Territories had been washed away. They were then re-scheduled to fly, but this also had to be cancelled. At 6.30 I held a sherry party for some 25 (Electoral) Returning Officers – but there was still no sign of the expected visitors. At long last, at nearly 11 p.m., the party of two MPs and three journalists (from the BBC, the *Daily Express* and *West Africa*), arrived. At 11 p.m. seven of us dined. The MPs stayed in the

Residency, and the others elsewhere in Kumasi. We went to bed late! The next day, as was to be expected, was a full one. There were meetings for the visitors with the NLM and the CPP, with my own officers, and with the Asantehene, and different persons came to lunch, tea, sherry, and dinner. Luckily I had a good Secretary, who acted as a most efficient ADC

The election was on 17th July. All day I visited polling booths, and in the evening went to Prempeh Hall with the MPs, to watch the counting. We dined at 9.30 (I have said earlier that the African cooks provided food at any hour and for any number, and this they truly did). The overall vote for Ghana was CPP, 69, and others, 33. The CPP won easily. But in Ashanti the NLM won 13 of the 21 seats.

A few days later, all being quiet in Ashanti, I drove down to Accra, and the next day flew home – still by that antiquated route, Kano-Tripoli-Rome-London. Leave was spent partly in Edinburgh and partly again at Kintail, which we all loved.

After two months, in October 1956, I set forth for what was to prove to be my last tour – the sixteenth. I sailed on 4th October, but the weather was so rough that we could not get into the Channel and stayed in Liverpool all day. Then, when we did sail, we met plenty of bad weather. A few days later we had great excitement as we closed in on a burning Spanish oil tanker. It was really very exciting, but the crew soon gained control, and we moved on. And so on to Freetown, where I had an early morning bathe in the ship's pool and then welcomed my sister to breakfast, went ashore with her, and after lunch returned to the ship. We sailed and reached Takoradi a few days later.

CHAPTER 17

Sixteenth and Last Tour:
October 1956 – May 1957

I went up to Kumasi as fast as I could drive. I stayed, for a change, in the Governor's Wing, as the Residency was being overhauled. After a week to settle down and assess the situation, I drove to Accra for meetings with the Governor and Prime Minister, and while in Accra I laid the foundation stone of the Ridge Church School.

This was to be my last tour. It was a short one, but exciting from start to finish. The Ashantis realised that Nkrumah and the CPP were pressing for Independence as soon as possible. Nkrumah was very anti-Ashanti – anti-Chief in general, and anti-Asantehene in particular – and the Ashantis felt that they were on their last legs. So from time to time we had excitement, but for most of the time work (and play) went on as usual. Certainly at times I was busy, often late at night, but I had as much golf as usual and certainly enough 'socialising' – for Ashanti was to be inundated with VIPs.

On 11th November we had the usual Armistice Day parade, and at the end I took the salute, as was customary. It was probably another nail in my coffin as far as Nkrumah was concerned. Next day there was a hockey match – the Gold Coast versus Nigeria. I greeted the teams and later presented the trophy. Then two days later, two representatives from the World Bank arrived. They also stayed with me and I held another sherry party (some 25 guests) for them. Later in the month, in uniform, I took the salute of the Passing Out Parade of Regimental Cadets, and in the afternoon attended some College Sports, I being 'Patron', and presented the trophies. Later the same day I had friends in to sherry and dinner ere going to some party in the late evening of which I was also a patron.

Early in December I actually had a quiet day – my diary records it, so it was probably the only quiet day in this whole tour. On 7th December I was woken at 3.30 a.m., left Kumasi at four, and reached Accra at 8, when kind friends gave me breakfast. Then I attended a three-hour meeting, discussing Independence 'Celebrations.' I listened to the proposals for Accra, and was asked for mine for Kumasi. (As yet I had none, but later set up and chaired a 36 member committee to plan them: they were to prove a great success.) After a quick lunch I drove back to Kumasi in time for a Golf Committee meeting (I being president), and finally a dinner at the large and well run Wesley College – there were 400 of us at dinner. Then the following morning, at eight prompt, I drove west to Sunyani (80 miles), where I cut the tape and opened new District Council Offices. This was followed by champagne with the Chairman. It was just as well I liked champagne, for it seemed to appear on numerous occasions.

The next entertainment was a sherry party for my Administrative officers, that is, District Commissioners, 24 in all. A few days later I was pleased to re-visit my happy hunting ground, Wenchi, to open an Agricultural Show. And so to Christmas. My diary records that I received 164 Christmas cards, locally. And then, being alone, my wife waiting till after the Christmas holidays to join me, I went into hiding in Kintampo for four or five days. This rest must have been bliss.

I returned to Kumasi for the New Year, 1957 and there was great excitement as my honour – CMG – was in the local and the UK press. I was swamped with letters and telegrams of congratulation. In my earlier days Chief Commissioners expected the CMG and often higher, a knight-hood, but by 1950 there were more senior officers at Gold Coast head-quarters, and the Chief Commissioners of Ashanti and the Northern Territories usually received the CMG. But this would be the last time for this, as two or three months later the post of Chief Commissioner (or rather, Chief Regional Officer) was abolished by Nkrumah – and I am not sure if, today, Ghanaians are permitted to receive honours.

Next some minor happenings. I was made Chairman of the Ashanti Dining Club. I had Sir Arku Korsah, the Chief Justice, to stay, and he was followed by Lord Hastings, who, like so many of my guests, was here to see how the Gold Coast was behaving. I worshipped again in the Methodist Church – a shorter service, only two hours this time.

In the middle of January, 1957, I was required urgently at Government House to discuss the forthcoming visit of Alan Lennox-Boyd, Secretary of State, who was coming to see for himself whether Ghana was truly fit for Independence or whether there would be too much rioting or bloodshed. Apart from having a three-hour meeting with the Governor and many others, life in Accra seemed to be not unlike that in Kumasi. After the meeting I was at a sherry party, then a dinner party, and finally a dance in the town. Next day I flew back to Kumasi (who would have believed such happenings when I first landed in 1929), and in the afternoon attended the opening of a new Secondary School – and gave the speech, '25 Years Progress.'

The next excitement (and it really was exciting) was the visit to Kumasi of the Secretary of State for the Colonies, Alan Lennox-Boyd. The purpose was for him to see the nature and strength of feeling in Ashanti (or at least in Kumasi). And he certainly saw it. I met him at the airport at 9.30 a.m. He had arrived from Accra. Normally both the Governor and the Prime Minister would have accompanied such a senior UK official, but the Ashantis were so hostile to Nkrumah and also to the Governor (who, they thought, was, if anything, encouraging Nkrumah) that they decided not to come and risk what would probably be a very large disturbance.

Kumasi, visit of Secretary of State

Kumasi, the crowds at the Secretary of State's visit

We drove first to greet the Asantehene and the Asanteman Council, and never have the streets of Kumasi been so crowded. Lennox-Boyd was travelling in my car, which was flying, as usual, a Union Jack. (All District Commissioners flew the Union Jack on the bonnets of their cars, but only in their own Districts). Not only was the crowd immense but it was orderly and ably controlled by the police. As Nkrumah could not come, a senior CPP follower was designated to meet the Secretary of State. He was travelling in a car close behind mine. Once I looked round and saw an enthusiastic NLM, who had been cheering us, suddenly realise who was in the second car. Quick as lightning, he bent down, picked up a handful of gravel, and hurled it at the CPP car. The official estimate was that the road was lined by from 50,000 to 100,000 people.

We met the Asanteman Council at 9.45 a.m. and, after a couple of formal speeches, we continued to the Residency. It was 10.30 so I offered Lennox-Boyd a coffee. He asked for gin and never have I seen anyone deserve it more. He had, only two days previously, come from Kenya, where the Mau Mau was at its height, and where he had been meeting officials and others. Yet here he was, only a few days later, fully briefed with the Ghana situation, knowing in full the Ashanti problem.

From 10.30 to 12.30 in the Residency, Lennox-Boyd met a delegation from the NLM Then my wife provided us with lunch. In the afternoon, from 3 to 4, he met the Administrative Officers of Ashanti, and from 4 to 5.30 representatives of the Asanteman Council. Then he had half an hour with the CPP I provided a sherry party of 43, next a brief half hour to change, and then a dinner party for 14 of us. These included the Asantehene, Essumajahene (senior chief in Ashanti), and an African Judge and his wife. Lennox-Boyd was accompanied by his wife and two senior Colonial Office officials.

This was 26th January. We closed just ere midnight, but I was up at five the next morning, trying to draft some clauses for the Ghana Independence Act (soon to go before Parliament). Lennox-Boyd and his staff were also up early, engaged in the same pursuit. Breakfast was at seven, then I had a full hour with Lennox-Boyd, next a quick glass of champagne with the Asantehene, and at 11, after exactly 25 hours in Ashanti, Lennox-Boyd's party left for Tamale. My wife and I then enjoyed relaxing with lunch in the Regimental Mess – followed by another call on the Asantehene.

Lennox-Boyd's visit to the Northern Territories was as brief as to Ashanti, for the following day I flew to Accra for another meeting with him and the Governor. I spent the next day in Accra still trying to produce a suitable amendment to the proposed Constitution – one that would please both the Ashantis and Nkrumah. The Ashanti did not want a Federal Constitution – or if they did, they realised that this was a non-starter. But they did want some safeguards in the Constitution for both Chiefs in general and especially for the Asanteman Council. We all worked on this, but at the back of our minds was Nkrumah's statement to some of his CPP, that if there was any part of the Constitution not to his liking, he would tear it up the day after Independence (and I believed that this he would have done).

After returning to Kumasi, we had another sherry party of 65 and then Elma and I had a few days off to visit Tamale (240 miles north). We stayed with the Chief Commissioner there – we were the last two Chief Regional Officers in Ghana, and by a coincidence my daughter and his daughter later shared rooms at St Andrew's University.

A fortnight later Baffuor Akoto, one of the Asantehene's chief linguists or spokesmen, and also a very prominent NLM, came to see me just to say 'Thank you.' Another sherry party of 50. In case readers wonder why I did not go broke, I was in receipt of an entertainment allowance of £350 per annum, and whisky was still only 12s. a bottle. Also when I considered that any party had gone on long enough, I would withdraw – a signal for guests to take their departure. They were not forced to go, but no more drinks would be forthcoming so obviously they left.

My next guest was General Sir Edward Spears, and for him a small sherry party of 18. And before that party I had again been to Bekwai with a few friends to seek the Colobus monkey and we had been fortunate. We saw the white-tailed, but only five of them. Like the world over, the forest was being cut and there were less trees for the monkeys – a world-wide problem.

And so to March. On the 1st March Lord Hemingford, whom I had known as Denis Herbert at Oxford, called. The next day I took a parade by the Ghana Police and presented a dozen medals. I suppose this would have annoyed Nkrumah, who would feel that a CPP should have been invited to do so. The same afternoon Elma presented trophies in connection with the celebration parties. On the 3rd we had a rehearsal on Fort Field. The Fort Field was not without meaning. It was adjoining the old Kumasi Fort where, in 1900, the Governor, Sir Frederick Hodgson, had been imprisoned for almost three months by the Ashantis till relieved by British troops from Tamale. There were many open spaces in and around Kumasi, which had been well laid out with, for example, two golf courses, a race course, polo field, school playing fields and soccer fields for anyone. But the Fort Field was in the centre of the town and had great significance for Europeans as well as Africans. And here was where the Union Flag was to be pulled down at midnight.

On the 4th of March, 1957, Lord Portal and several others came in for a beer before lunch and General Spears and others came for lunch. In the afternoon there was a rehearsal for the post-Independence parade, but I was still fit enough to play four games of squash in the evening. Malaria had been not a killer with me, but very debilitating for many, many years. But now I seemed to have thrown it off, and in consequence resumed my normal good health.

Tuesday, 5th March, was a public holiday. The Secretary of State sent a final message to the NLM and to the Asantehene – very much appreciated. We had no trouble, but in Togoland things were bad. Southern Togoland was mandated to the UK after World War I and had wished

Kumasi, the Fort

to leave the Gold Coast and join their kin in French Togoland, which was to become the present-day Togo. But we counted on the votes in Northern Togoland, which wished to remain part of the Northern Territories, and overall there was a majority for remaining part of Ghana. Nevertheless, trouble was to be expected and trouble there was – but soon overcome.

At 6 p.m. the Quarter-guard came to pull down the Union Flag at the Residency. I almost wept, for although I had been working for nearly 30 years for this to happen – undoubtedly our object – when it happened, it was sad to see our beloved Union Jack taken down for the last time. I still have that flag. Later, in uniform of course, I went down to the Fort Field, and at 11.45 p.m. the Union Flag was ceremonially lowered. Then, exactly at midnight, the Ghana Flag was hoisted.

I then returned to the Residency and with my number two was drinking beer. Surprisingly, at about two a.m., the telephone rang. I answered it. It was the well known croaky voice of Baffuor Akoto. "Is that Your Honour? I'm free now. Ha! Ha! Ha!," and he put down the receiver. One of the bravest telephone calls I've ever received. He knew he would be in prison soon, and sure enough he was imprisoned probably several times. Thank the Lord, prisoners were not badly treated, though Baffuor Akoto did not know that when he rang me.

Eventually I got to bed, but was up early the next morning for the official Ashanti Independence Celebrations. At 8.30 a.m., in uniform, I was in the Prince of Wales Park, to find there a large gathering of Chiefs – no less than 70 of them, each with his umbrella, drums, horns, and followers, etc., etc., and some 4,500 school children. All the stands were full of Europeans and Africans, a total crowd of about 20,000. After I had taken the salute (Gold Coast Police), I greeted the Chiefs. I then gave an address, lasting some ten minutes, referring to the fact that the Gold Coast was now Ghana. The school children then marched past and this took 35 minutes. Everything passed off quietly except for a few scuffles that were inevitable. The Commanding Officer, Regimental Depot, had parked his squad about five miles beyond Kumasi, but each time there was a scuffle he moved the squad closer. Luckily, they were not needed. In fact the parade passed off better than anyone could have hoped or expected. After it was over, I returned to the Residency and some five or six of my officers and Baffuor Akoto joined me for a well deserved beer. Next day there was a Carnival Procession when Elma robed the Beauty Queen, and in the evening we attended the Asantehene's Reception for nearly 700 guests.

Next day, the 8th, it was my turn, and after receiving a continuous influx of VIPs – including Canadians and Poles – I gave a garden party for about 450. This was followed by the four Canadians and several others staying on to sherry ere I went to another sherry party given by the Kumasi Chamber of Commerce. On the 9th, accompanied by the Regimental Depot Commander, Colonel Hewitt, in white uniform as usual, we drove to Mampong – one of the largest Ashanti Divisions – where there was a full-scale Durbar, some 6,000 present. In the afternoon I received four Burmese at the Residency, then attended the race meeting and presented the Independence trophy. After that I was really able to relax, playing a few games of squash in the Army squash court.

Next day, back to celebrations again. There was a huge fireworks display in the evening, watched by Elma, Bridget and myself. £1,000 of fireworks were used – quite a lot of money in those days. I then had a dinner party, 14 of us, including the local African Judge and the three Burmese who were staying at the Residency, after which we all went to the Independence Ball till maybe three a.m. or so. On the next two days there were several sherry parties each night, and I had two Czechs to stay.

One day Elma and I attended Pontifical High Mass in the Roman Catholic Cathedral – ushered in by men in uniform carrying wooden swords. I think the service was probably about three hours, but after an hour one of these sword-bearing officers came formally up to me and said, "You may now leave, sir," which we did. Later that day, to my great joy, Sir Alan Burns (to whom I had been Private Secretary twice, in Accra and also in Lagos) arrived to stay. I had a large dinner party that night, as usual about half Ghanaian. Certainly we had made arrangements for 'Independence Celebration,' and they worked well. It seemed as though all Kumasi wished to take part, and night after night we attended sherry parties when we were not ourselves entertaining. A few days later Sir Robert Jackson (Volta River) called, and later again I had a dinner party of 16, including the Principal of Kumasi College of Technology, and I was at his College on some Committee for ten hours the next day – excessive!

On 29th March Catherine arrived out for her short Easter holidays and Margaret arrived a few days later. I was delighted to have my whole family with me to see part of the Celebrations.

So to April. It began with the Cabinet abolishing the post of Chief Regional Officer. Actually, I think this was correct. What I had been doing was quite distinctively as a Civil Servant on behalf of the Governor. But henceforth the Governor would be purely ceremonial, and the CRO's work would be on behalf of the Prime Minister and should therefore be a political appointment. To me personally, and to MacDonald-Smith in the Northern Territories, it was not too distressing, since we were both thinking of retiring in any case. None the less, it was disappointing to learn that one's post was no more, all without any prior discussion or warning. And (almost comical), the next day I took the Oath of Allegiance and the Judicial Oath – to be followed by champagne – from Judge Manyo-Plange, who had often been at my dinner and sherry parties.

Immediately on Independence, as was to be expected, the Governor, Sir Charles Arden-Clarke, was promoted by the Queen to the rank and title of Governor-General. And now that Independence had been granted, the NLM were no longer fighting other than through the ballot box, so that the Governor-General was free to visit Kumasi. On 7th April, as was customary, I drove to the limit of my jurisdiction, the frontier of Ashanti, the bridge over the River Prah where, sixty-one years earlier, Baden-Powell had been ferried over from the Colony into Ashanti. I met the Governor-General. I took him to call on the Asantehene, and then we were entertained at a sherry party in the Officers' Mess before HE, having "taken over" the Residency, gave a dinner party in the evening, to be followed the next evening by his sherry party for 300, also at the Residency.

Soon after, the Asantehene called on me one evening to present Elma with a silk Kente cloth – a really gorgeous and neatly hand-woven piece of craftsmanship. The next day, accompanied by Margaret (then aged 14), I drove to Kintampo to entertain the station to a sherry party, and the next day I attended the opening of the Kintampo Health Centre, done correctly by a Cabinet Minister and not by me.

On 15th April I had a day-long meeting with my District Commissioners, now to be called Government Agents – GAs. This too was correct. We were no longer Officers of the Crown, but subordinate 'agents' of the Government in power (though it was unfortunate that the African tribe in Accra were known as Ga, so that the DC Accra, became the GaGa!). After the day long meeting, I gave them and their wives, and also General Paley, Commanding Gold Coast Troops, a sherry party for 25 of us.

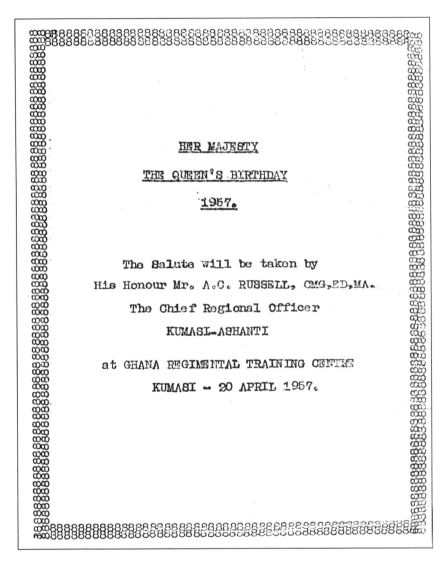

HER MAJESTY

THE QUEEN'S BIRTHDAY

1957.

The Salute will be taken by

His Honour Mr. A.C. RUSSELL, CMG,ED,MA.

The Chief Regional Officer

KUMASI-ASHANTI

at GHANA REGIMENTAL TRAINING CENTRE

KUMASI - 20 APRIL 1957.

Above, and following pages: Order of Parade, the Queen's Birthday Parade, 20th April, 1957

ORDER   OF   PARADE

6735   Parade will march on.

0750   Parade will be taken over by
            Commanding Officer.

0800   C.R.O. arrives on Parade

            C.R.O. Inspects the Parade
            The Parade marches past in SLOW
            and QUICK TIME.

            The Parade rejoins Line and gives
            the ROYAL Salute representing the
            arrival of Her Majesty.

            The Parade advances in Review Order
                followed by Ghana National
                Anthem

            The Parade give 3 cheers for H.M.
                The Queen followed by Second
                ROYAL Salute representing the
                Salute to the Queen on leaving
                the Parade followed by Ghana
                National Anthem.

            The Officer Commanding GRTC requests
                permission to march off.

            OOOOOOOOOOOOOOOOOOOO

Action by Parade.	by Spectators.
Received with ROYAL Salute	Stand - UNCOVER Sit down.
The C.R.O. takes the Salute.	
The C.R.O. leaves the Saluting Dias and moves to a position to a flank and faces the Flagstaff	Stand and uncover "
The C.R.O. remounts the Saluting Dias after the 2nd Royal Salute	"
The C.R.O. moves to a new saluting base opposite 30x Range and the Parade marches off in divisions.	Sit down.

ooooooooooooooooooooooo

OFFICERS ON PARADE.

Officer Commanding Parade

      LT.COL. A.G. HEWITT, MBE, MC.

NO. 1 GD. 2/LT M.T. CHRISTIAN-EDWARDS

NO. 2 GD. 2/LT D.C. BENSON

NO. 3 GD. 2/LT *G.A.* MEDAWAR

NO. 4 GD. 2/LT A.P. ARCHIBALD

NO. 5 GD. 2/LT D.M. LONGLEY

PARADE RSM.

RSM OSEINI BAZABARIMI, BEM.

Kumasi, the Race Course. Asantehene with Mrs. Russell and self

On 18th April there was a rehearsal for the Queen's Birthday Parade, which was two days later. There, rightly or wrongly, I took the salute in front of Colonel Hewitt, five subalterns, and 220 men. This was the last time such a parade was held in Ghana. Ghana was to become a Republic. I treasure the Order of Parade which Colonel Hewitt, now in Queensland, presented to me many years later (see previous pages).

On 24th April we had Bridget's birthday party for 19 children. On 26th April the Kumasi Municipal Council was suspended. I suppose they were all NLM and Nkrumah wished for fresh elections. That evening the Ghana Police, at their Kumasi Depot, 'beat retreat,' and when I left the Band played 'The Queen' even though this was now contrary to Government orders. Needless to say, I had not asked for this but it was customary, it had always been done, so it seemed natural – especially as the Police Officers would be true servants of the Queen as well as of Nkrumah.

One evening I visited the Kumasi Race Course to see the stables. I counted some 170 horses, and was told that the value of many was £600

PRIME MINISTER

16th October, 1956.

Dear Mr Russell,

   Thank you very much for your letter of the
3rd October.

   May I say welcome back and may I also express the
hope that you have a successful and a happier tour this
time. The past few months have not been easy for any of
us and we hope the discussions which begin today with the
Opposition will lead to a satisfactory solution of our
present problem.

   There is nothing urgent that I would like to discuss
with you but I shall certainly be pleased to have a chat with
you when you are in Accra on the 26th October, preferably in
the morning, say round about 10.30.

   With kindest regards to you and Mrs. Russell,

Yours sincerely,
Kwame Nkrumah

A. C. Russell, Esq., E.D.

Letter from the Prime Minister, Kwame Nkrumah

and some even £2,000 – a lot of money in those days. Even more remarkable was keeping horses in the tsetse belt, but maybe as Kumasi was full of people and few trees, the tsetse fly no longer dwelt there. The next day another MP, Mr C. J. M. Alport, came to stay, and I had a sherry party for 90.

And so to May, my last month. It began with Elma driving Margaret and Catherine to Accra, to fly home after their Easter holidays. On 8th May the ominous telegram arrived from the Prime Minister that he wished to see me the following morning. So, rising early, I left at 5 a.m. and drove to Accra, had breakfast with a friend, and at 11.15 appeared before the Cabinet. The meeting lasted an hour. I always say that I was 'sacked,' but this is not strictly true. The Cabinet were, on the whole, polite; indeed, very polite. Only one or two with whom I had had 'difficulties' were at all brusque, but most of them I knew well and we had worked amicably together. I have stated earlier that Nkrumah trusted me even though our policies differed. A good example of his courtesy is the letter he wrote to me on my return to Kumasi for my last tour (see preceeding page). Nkrumah knew that while I obeyed him, my sympathies were still Ashanti. Basically, the Cabinet confirmed that not only was the post of Chief Regional Officer to be abolished, but announced the final decision that I must quit Ashanti (Kumasi) within a week. I was to be found other work to do.

I immediately accepted the fact that I had to leave Kumasi and, not wishing for a post elsewhere, decided to take the first boat home. First, however, I went to Government House to tell the Governor-General, and then to Elder Dempster to see if they could give me (and Elma and Bridget) a cabin and a passage home soon. Then I drove back to Kumasi. Elma was not displeased. Indeed, she was pleased to think that we might live nearer to our children and live in our own and not a 'tied' house.

Elder Dempster had a boat in a fortnight, and this fortnight was to be really hectic. The next day it began when we had the BNCOs (British Non-Commissioned Officers) with their wives and children to tea. Next day it was a sherry party by the Asantehene for 600. The next party was by my Administrative Officers, then once more to Accra to say farewell to the Governor-General and to greet Sir Arku Korsah, Chief Justice, who succeeded him as Governor-General. On the 16th I was dined by the Officers' Mess, Kumasi. The next day the Asantehene's personal secretary brought me a gift from the Asantehene. It was an ivory cane, a beautiful piece of Kumasi craftsmanship. It unscrews (like modern billiard cues), and fits into a small box. It will be more than useful when my eyesight goes. Every day I gave a talk somewhere – Prempeh College, the International Club, and so on.

Next day the Asantehene held a mid-day sherry party (for 150). In the afternoon I presented the 'Gold Coast Badge and Certificate of Honour' to some worthy recipient, then to a sherry party given by the Sports Council (80 guests), and finally Elma and I were dined by the BNCO's Mess. But while Ghana was 'growing' fast, occasionally one had glimpses into the past, for example, from a BNCO: "I asked for a gin and anything, and she brought me a gin and a bar of chocolate." And my secretary's comment one day, to his great surprise: "Sir, this champagne is French."

On 17th May Dr Busia (later to be Prime Minister) called to say good-bye. The next day there was another sherry party by the Asantehene (150 guests). The Asantehene, knowing that I had refused any other post in Ghana after

At the Railway Station.

having been Chief Commissioner, Ashanti, said to me privately, "I'm proud of you." These were words which thrilled me. This is probably the place to say something about the contrast I felt between the Ashanti on the one hand and the Akan of the Colony on the other. I liked all the people of the Gold Coast, but unquestionably I had a fondness for many Ashantis. This dated back to my first days in Fomena in 1929, when Kobina Foli, the old Warrior Chief, felt that it was his duty, his responsibility, to make sure that I had what was needed and paid frequent visits to my Rest House. Later, in Wenchi, I have mentioned how the totally illiterate Wenchihene had tightly gripped my arm and pointed out where he had been chased by his enemies. These are just two examples of so many I remember. Yes, I liked the Gold Coasters in general, but had a particular affection for many of the Ashantis – and especially for the Asantehene himself. In the south I think the District Commissioner was looked on as one who kept law and order and gave out gunpowder permits and so forth. He was highly re-spected but was also held to be a bit of a nuisance! In Ashanti, by contrast, I sensed that the people liked our help and seemed to know that we were really trying to give them good advice and assistance.

On 20th May the Red Cross gave a party for Elma, and in the evening I gave a final sherry party for 150 before dining with the Ashanti Dining Club. And so to my last day in Kumasi. I was with the Asanteman Council for an hour, and this included making a presentation to them of a Chief's sacred chair that had been seized by the British in the 1896 expedition and was now being returned to them by the Secretary of State, Lennox-Boyd. I had the usual champagne with the Asantehene, then went back to the Residency. There were callers all day but I managed to make a short escape for a few games of squash. Elma and I dined, then one of my senior officers drove me, at 9 p.m., to the Railway Station. There I was greeted by a Guard of Honour from the Regiment playing their Silver Drums; also a drum band from the College of Technology; and a large number of Chiefs with their followers.

It was a sad moment, but at 10 p.m. the train departed, the last coach being for me, that is, for Elma, Bridget, myself, and cook. At Bekwai, when the train stopped, I found no less than five Head Chiefs and the two Government Agents on the platform to say farewell . . . and after that we retired to our beds.

Wednesday, 22nd of May, 1957. We arrived at Takoradi at 6 a.m. We

On the train. Bridget with Mrs. Russell and self

had a leisurely morning and a swim, and then at 3 p.m. boarded the MV *Accra*, where I received some 30 letters and telegrams. A large number of friends were there to say farewell. At 7 p.m. we sailed and I went on to the bridge with the Captain. As we passed the end of the jetty, I saw and heard and saluted the buglers of the Ghana Police playing 'The Hausa Farewell.' I can think of no finer farewell from the country I had come to love.

Appendices

Appendix I

Glossary

Ohene (or . . . hene)	Twi for Chief
Omanhene	Chief of a Division, or Head Chief
Asantehene	Paramount Chief, or King, of the Ashante
Bandahene	Head Chief of the Banda Division
Kyidomhene	Chief of the Rearguard
Odekro	Chief, or Headman, of a village
Linguist, or okyeame	Spokesman. A senior Chief does not speak in person publicly, but through his Linguist
Stool Throne.	On being elected, a Chief is enstooled. When no longer wanted by his subjects, he is destooled
Elders	Advisors of a Chief
'Young men'	Those who are not Chiefs, Sub-Chiefs or Elders
Nana	A deferential term, "grandfather" or "grandmother," used in addressing Chiefs
Zongo	A part of a town set apart for strangers, usually Northerners
Twi	The principal language of Ashanti and the

	Colony, of which Ashanti and Fante are the main dialects
H.E.	His Excellency, referring to the Governor
P. S. and A. D. C.	Private Secretary and Aide-de-Camp, usually working with the Governor
C.C.A./C.R.O.	Chief Commissioner (later Chief Regional Officer), Ashanti, usually referred to as "His Honour".
D. C.	District Commissioner (but in Nigeria, D. O. – District Officer), often referred to as "His Worship".
B. N. C. O.	British Non-Commissioned Officer

Family

Elma	My wife. We married in 1939
Margaret, Catherine, and Bridget	Our three daughters

Other relatives in West Africa:

My sister Margaret, married to Hugh Beattie, a District Commissioner in Sierra Leone

My cousin Arthur Russell, Gold Coast Forestry Service

My cousin Gina, wife of Governor Sir Charles Arden-Clarke

My cousin George Russell, Nigerian Forestry Service.

Appendix II

Ghana, formerly Gold Coast

Situation

West Africa. Latitude: in the tropic of cancer, between 5 and 11 degrees north of the Equator. Longitude: the Meridian of Greenwich lies just east of Accra.

In 1930 the Gold Coast consisted of:

A) The Gold Coast Colony, the southern part, administered by three Provincial Commissioners

B) Ashanti, the middle part, administered by a Chief Commissioner

C) The Northern Territories, the northern part, administered by a Chief Commissioner

D) Togoland, the eastern part, formerly German, but mandated after World War I to Great Britain and administered as part of the Gold Coast. The northern half was administered as part of the Northern Territories, and the southern half as part of the Colony.

Area

Gold Coast	92,000 square miles
Ashanti	25,000 square miles
Scotland	30,000 square miles

Population (to nearest 1,000)

	1930	1960	1984
Gold Coast	3,164,000	6,727,000	12,296,000
Ashanti (with Brong Ahafo)	579,000	1,697,000	3,297,000
Kumasi	36,000	218,000	490,000
Scotland (approx.)	5,000,000	5,000,000	5,000,000

Appendix III

Gold Coast/Ghana – Economic

Cocoa

The most valuable of Gold Coast products, amounting to about one-third world output. Cadburys, Unilever and many others involved. Grown in the forest country, that is all of Ghana except the littoral belt in the south and the savannah in the north.

Timber

Large exports of hardwood, mostly labelled "Mahogany" in the UK, but known locally as "Odum." Other varieties also exported. Source (as in the world generally) now diminishing, but thankfully many Forest Reserves were created by Government, where extraction was by licence only.

Mining

Gold is extensively mined. The famous and very rich ore at Obuasi is worked by the Ashanti Goldfields Corporation. There are many gold mines in the Tarkwa area.
There are also large deposits of bauxite and manganese.
Diamonds in the central part of the Colony are mined by a large company, much hampered by illicit operations.

Rubber

A little was produced, but now abandoned.

Oil Palm

None is produced commercially. Trees are common throughout the forest country, and are often used to produce palm wine.

Coconut Palm

No commercial production.

Fish

Plentiful supply along the Coast, every village having many boats (with paddle and sail). Today, there is a motorised fleet. All fish caught are immediately sun-dried.

Kola

Many trees in parts of Ashanti. Valuable export in olden times, when it was carried to the North by long lines of donkeys tied head to tail.

Food Crops

Generally plentiful, over all the country. During my 28 years service there was never a famine or shortage.

Budget

In 1930 the Gold Coast balanced its budget. Expenditure and revenue were each about L2 million, which seems ridiculously low by today's costs. Half the income came from the Customs Duty on gin (Dutch Schnapps), which cost 8s. a bottle in shops. It was used mainly on ceremonial occasions, and for pouring libations to ancestral spirits. Drunkenness was uncommon.

Appendix IV

Kit and Luggage

When we moved station, it was fortunate both that transport was arranged through the Public Works Department, and that our "boys" were first class at packing and never complained. In 1951, when I moved from Cape Coast to Accra, I noted that my "baggage" consisted of:

9 large boxes made at Jenners to transport our wedding presents abroad.
4 crates made at Juaso.
10 large mahogany (Odum) crates made by a timber firm in Kumasi.
3 small crates, from an Edinburgh grocer, for exporting tinned
foods to us.
3 "tea chests."
5 metal boxes (2 trunks, 1 uniform case, 2 helmet boxes).
4 tin boxes, deed boxes from my father.
2 tin baths, used on trek to hold blankets, bedding, etc.

4 tin boxes, miscellaneous.
1 44 – gallon drum, to hold petrol on long journeys.
1 4-gallon jerry can.
1 soda cylinder – 4 feet high, to hold gas for my sodastream. It
lasted for an 18-months' tour.
Also,
2 trunks
6 suit cases
2 hat boxes (for Elma's hats)
3 golf bags
1 sewing machine
3 bicycles
2 prams
2 camp beds
1 refrigidaire
2 carpets
2 tables, for use on trek
4 deck chairs
4 miscellaneous pieces

And in addition, as in 1951, when collecting for Edinburgh Zoo, another
20 miscellaneous pieces – aviaries, cages, etc.

Gross Total: say, 120 pieces.

Appendix V

Edinburgh Zoo

Between 1946 and 1957 I sent ten consignments of livestock to Edinburgh
Zoo. Eight of these went by sea and two by air. Only twice did I accompany
the consignments, and I must pay tribute to the great helpfulness of the
ships' and air crews, port authorities, Gold Coast Railways, and others. I
received help from everyone involved. Here are the details of one such
consignment: 1 baboon, 1 chimpanzee, 8 monkeys (of 4 varieties), 6 birds
of prey (3 varieties), 5 animals (3 varieties), 20 doves, etc. (9 varieties), 38

miscellaneous birds (12 varieties), 1 snake: in all, 80 livestock. In total I sent several hundred birds and several hundred animals, but only a few reptiles. Elma did not approve of my collecting snakes.

These were collected in various ways, principally by road labourers in my employ (sometimes as many as 150), encouraged by a most helpful overseer; and by village Chiefs letting it be known what the District Commissioner's strange habits were. At times I employed as many as three keepers, and in addition, before a shipment, a carpenter to make suitable crates for the voyage.

All livestock was kept for several weeks (or even months) to make sure it survived in captivity. This proved beneficial, since few died either en route or when reaching Edinburgh. My costs were considerable, but were reimbursed by the Zoo.

Briefly, I sent:

Animals

Duiker (small antelopes) – 4 varieties
Monkey – 4 varieties
2 baboons
1 chimpanzee
Squirrel – 3 varieties
Pottos and Bush Babies – small nocturnal animals.

Birds

Owls – 4 varieties
Hawks – 5 varieties
Eagle – 2 of the magnificent Crowned Hawk-Eagle, whose favourite food was monkey lifted from the tree tops
Touraco – many; brightly coloured, larger than a cuckoo
Plantain-eater – both the brightly coloured and the plain
Hornbill – 2 varieties
Pigeons and Doves – many varieties
Golden Oriole – 4
Finches (small birds) – several hundred, many varieties.

Brief notes on my collecting activities may be read in:

Nigerian Field Society, vol. XIV, No. 1, January 1949.

Edinburgh Zoo Magazine, "Scottish Zoo and Wild Life,"
Vols. I, Oct. 1948, and II, April 1949.

Appendix VI

gifts received

During my last ten days in the Gold Coast, amidst almost continuous
farewell parties, etc., the following gifts were received:-

Nana Otumfuo Prempeh II, King of Ashanti:	*ivory cane, with gold rings*
The Kumasi Sports Club:	*elaborate gold cuff links, (Ashanti Stool and Ceremonial Sword)*
Ashanti Dining Club:	*canteen of cutlery (now in daily use with Bridget, in Queensland)*
The College of Technology:	*set of 6 beer mugs and 6 bowls, locally made*
Akyempimhene:	*gold tie pin (engraved ACR)*
Ashanti Farmers' Union:	*gold brooch*
Prempeh College:	*2 miniature Ivory Stools and a wooden bowl*
Abanasehene:	*model of the head of the late Ejisuhene, silvered*
Road Overseer, Akadom:	*table cloth*
The ex-Adansihene:	*4 ornamental wooden fruit bowls, locally made*
Essumajahene:	*set of table mats*
Ashanti Cultural Centre:	*miniature ceremonial sword (gold plated)*
Ben Tamakloe, Solicitor:	*ivory lamp,*

and from my District
Commissioners:

large silver Quaich, which sits permanently on my dining table.

and to Elma

Nana Otumfuo Prempeh II:

2 pieces of Kente cloth, silk, gorgeous colours, hand woven

Ashanti Sports Council:

ivory bracelet

The Lutterodts (traders):

ivory bracelet

The Red Cross:

gold brooch (large, "Ashanti Red Cross")

Akyempimhene:

gold brooch

The College of Technology:

2 pieces of cloth (local, hand woven)

J. W. Poku (my Clerk):

necklace.

Appendix VII

political report

REGIONAL OFFICE,
PO Box 38,
KUMASI, ASHANTI

SECRET   2nd January

Sir,

SECURITY APPRECIATION: ASHANTI

A meeting was held in my office on the afternoon of 31st December. There is little change in the situation. The Opposition are placing great hopes on a visit from the Secretary of State – they seem to know more about the Secretary of State's movements than Government Officers, they clearly believe the Secretary of State <u>will</u> pay a visit to the Gold Coast.

The NLM directive that there should be no violence still stands; in fact they have gone out of their way to provide as little provocation as possible. CPP flags have appeared in many parts of Ashanti; several Ministers have been visiting Ashanti and other visits are contemplated; and RR Amponsah's car was burnt on the 30th December. None of these acts has invited retaliation. This in our opinion does not mean any weakening amongst the ranks of the NLM supporters though undoubtedly the Prime Minister is likely to infer that the CPP are in greater strength in Ashanti than is the case.

At the meeting we discussed the loss of 75,000 cartridges, in the ownership of the CFAO, which disappeared between Takoradi and Wenchi. The Assistant Commissioner of Police is tightening up the procedure regarding transit of arms and ammunition into and through Ashanti. In this connection it is rumoured that there is gun-running on a large scale into Western Ashanti from the Ivory Coast but this has not been confirmed.

Colonel Harrison informed us that owing to France increasing the rate of recruitment in the French Colonial Forces, he is not able to recruit the number of men required from the Northern Territories (or adjoining

French possessions) and that his rate of recruitment may be reduced from two platoons to half a platoon monthly. If this situation continues for long, results will be serious.

My assessment is that the NLM are unwilling to cause any trouble so long as there is a possibility of mediation. I think they will not even be provoked if more CPP flags are displayed and with visits from Cabinet Ministers; it is even possible that action with the Brongs might not provoke them but here we are getting into the realm of speculation.

At the meeting, as a result of discussion, I have issued orders that all Government Agents will hold regular weekly meetings with the senior police officer in the District and will send me regular weekly reports on the security situation in their District.

I have the honour to be

Sir,

Your obedient Servant

A.C.RUSSELL

THE SECRETARY TO THE GOVERNOR,
GOVERNMENT HOUSE,
ACCRA

CHIEF REGIONAL OFFICER
copy to: Major R. N. M
Milton, Min. of the Inter
Asst. Commr. Police/
Ashanti (2)
HH The Chief Regional
Officer, NTs